# PAST THE HOOD ORNAMENT

*life through the rearview mirror*

# PAST THE HOOD ORNAMENT

*life through the rearview mirror*

*by*

# Mike Carmichael

WordCrafts

**Past The Hood Ornament**
 *life through the rearview mirror*
Copyright © 2014
Michael Carmichael

Cover design by David Warren
Cover photo by Don Keefe

All rights reserved. No part of this book may be reproduced, stored in a retrieval system, or transmitted in any form or by any means – electronic, mechanical, photocopy, recording, or otherwise – without the prior written permission of the publisher. The only exception is brief quotations for review purposes.

Published by WordCrafts Press
Tullahoma, TN 37388
www.wordcrafts.net

# DEDICATION

Without a lot of help and encouragement this book would not be possible. Two very special people I owe a tremendous thank you are Paul Bergstrom and Don Keefe. I owe them so much and count them as friends.

The many members of the Pontiac Oakland Club International who have taken these writings to heart. I appear in the club publication monthly and am most honored by the privilege. All I do is write down memories. Thank you for allowing me to share them.

I thank my daughter, Heather and son-in-law Chad for putting up with me.

Finally, but not least, I thank my friend Mrs. Wiggins.

Thank you all so very much. God bless.

# TABLE OF CONTENTS

## FIRST GEAR
Stumping with my Brother .................................................. 2
I Love the LucyMobile ....................................................... 7
The Angel and McFonzie ................................................. 12
Uncle Miltie's On............................................................... 17
Salon Chez Debbie ........................................................... 21
Elves, Hearses, and Rainbows Over the Hills ........ 26
Reading Is Fundamental ................................................. 31
Big Red's Produce............................................................. 36
The Plumber's Friend ...................................................... 42
XY Squared Over WD 40................................................ 47

## SECOND GEAR
Pretty in Pink..................................................................... 53
Doctor, Lawyer, Indian Chief........................................ 58
Ian and the Disappearing Morris ............................... 63
GT...J?................................................................................... 68
The Homefront Chief....................................................... 72
One Fast Hair Dryer ........................................................ 77
Barney.................................................................................. 81

## THIRD GEAR
The Boss's Daughter ....................................................... 87
The Grand Farewell ......................................................... 92
Field of Dreams................................................................. 96
Here's to You, Mrs. Robinson..................................... 100
Coffee and Doughnuts in the Parking Lot ........... 105
Lunch Break Resto ......................................................... 109
Will She Run?.................................................................. 114

## FOURTH GEAR
The Partsman's Backyard ........................................... 121
The Cat Wagon ............................................................... 126
Saturday in the Park .................................................... 130

Scooby and the Mystery Machine......................... 135
Your Money, or I'll Shut It Off................................ 139
In Good Hands........................................................... 144
About the Author....................................................... 148

*life through the rearveiw mirror*

# FIRST GEAR

*Past the Hood Ornament*

## *Stumping with my Brother*

I remember the summer I turned six. I was excited about school. A few more months and I would start the first grade. In the meantime, I played with my friends and my older brother. The only problem is that my brother, Nick, is seven years older than me. He was, of course, twice my size, and, unlike me, he played little league baseball. He did not necessarily want to be stuck with me.

The times Nick and I were, in his words, stuck together, were far and few between. I turned six in 1955, the year when westerns were popular on TV. My brother would do really dumb things, and then try to blame me. Only, it would backfire on him. For example, remember the movie "A Christmas Story", where the kid begs Santa for a Red Ryder BB gun? Well, my parents gave one to Nick. One day, the two of us were in the backyard. Nick hung a tin can from a tree limb and was shooting at it. It went well for a while. And then he missed. Missed the can, but not Dad's 1954 Ford station wagon. The rear window looked like a spider web. Nick handed the Red Ryder to me and took off running. He rounded the corner of the garage and ran into Dad.

Dad saw me holding the BB gun and looked around, figuring something must be up. Seeing the Ford, he tightened his grip on my brother. Attempts to blame me only made Dad more angry. He knew I was too scrawny to cock the Red Ryder and he knew my brother would never let me near his precious BB gun.

Where Nick messed up was in his lie. Had he told the truth, he would have been all right. No, that was not to be. As a result, there was weeping and gnashing of teeth.

Then there was the time Nick and I were playing Cowboys and Indians. (This was 1955. I have no idea what they would call the game today.) He tied me up and put me in the back seat of Mom's car - in the garage. I was there four hours before Mom came looking for me. One more time, weeping and gnashing of teeth.

This next one was a whopper. My grandmother was with my parents, and her lovely '52 Pontiac was in the driveway. They had all left, leaving Nick in charge. My brother and I were watching television. After a while, he became bored and started looking for something to do. He went from room to room in search of some sort excitement. As I was watching cartoons, he yelled at me to come with him. He was heading out the back door as I caught up with him. All he would tell me was that l had to come with him because he promised Mom he would watch me. He had found the keys to the aforementioned Pontiac. It made no difference that I did not want to get in. He assured me we were only going to go for a ride around the pasture on the other side of the backyard. So, I got in. There were no seat belts. I held onto the armrest as Nick started the straight-eight, bringing it to an idle.

Then we were off. He seemed to do OK when you consider he was a few months short of thirteen years old. The old Chieftain crossed the backyard and into the pasture. It was empty space, nothing but an empty field for roughly an acre. The land was unused, belonging to the city, which would periodically mow the lot.

At the time of our great adventure, the grass was as tall as the car's bumpers. Nick wheeled around the field. For close to ten minutes we did figure eights and imaginary laps through the grass. Every now and then, he would get sideways, bumping and bouncing, which I found entertaining.

After a while, Nick decided that he'd had enough fun and was about to head back to the house. From one far corner, he cut the wheel and aimed the silver gray sedan diagonally toward the backyard. With my brother laughing maniacally, we picked up speed. I thought the bumping and bouncing was amusing, and joined in-briefly.

We had begun to slow, with maybe seventy-five feet to go until we reached our property line, when everything stopped. Literally. It was as though we hit a wall. I flew off the seat and onto the dash, coming to rest on the floor. I could hear my brother cursing and trying to restart the car, to no avail. Not only had the Titanic struck an iceberg, it had sunk!

I got up and opened my door. Time to bail! My brother was in front of the car, trying to find out the reason for all of this. It seems that in that whole acre of land Nick had found the only tree stump! The car had come to rest with the oil pan on the stump and the front wheels were off the ground. I took off on a run toward the house. It was a tense couple of hours, waiting for my parents to get home.

I had never seen my brother sweat so much! Of course, he was scared to death, and he took it out on me. He yelled. He pleaded with me. I think he even said something about running away.

I looked in the mirror and couldn't believe what I saw. My forehead had a large knot and a rapidly spreading purple bruise. I knew Dad would be furious, but I knew Dad would have to wait in line once my Mom got a look at me. Nick was up the proverbial creek without proper mode of transport.

Well, finally our parents came home. Mom took a look at me and hit the roof. Dad asked what had happened to me, and the story unraveled! First, Mom tore him up. Then Grandma tore him up. Then Dad marched him out to where the Pontiac was. Of course, Mom, Grandma and I followed. Dad looked at the car and pursed his lips. He looked at the car, then at my brother.

Now, Dad was a weightlifter and was very stout. He went over to Nick and put his left arm around his waist. He picked him up and inverted him. His bottom was up! Dad wailed on that bottom for ten minutes. He then told my brother to go to his room, which he wisely did. My mom and I followed.

Twenty minutes later, Dad came in and marched straight toward Nick's room. We could hear my brother getting beat. No, no, no. He wasn't beaten; he was beat. At one time, parents would whip their kids and cause them to repent, which is, I am pretty sure, what my brother did.

Dad had to get a tow truck to get the car off the stump. The car had to have a tie rod replaced as well as the oil pan, which was badly dented. Nick was placed on "house arrest," grounded, and the only thing he had to do with cars for a long time was washing them.

My brother was pretty nice to me for the next year and a half, until the day he was involved in a fight at school. So he begged my parents for permission to take martial arts lessons. They agreed. He threw his efforts into practicing. He would later go on to be an instructor in the military, but for the time being, I was miserable.

He would use me for his sparing partner, whether I wanted to or not. For the first six months or so, Dad was constantly pulling Nick off of me. l am surprised that social services did not come to the house, as I was usually bruised. But I decided to go with it. Whether I wanted to or not, I was learning to fight, to defend myself. This would become useful later on in life.

By the time he graduated, Nick was close to being a black belt. I never tried for belts; to me, it was self-defense, both from my brother and in general. Between weightlifting with my dad and fighting with my brother, I was in pretty good shape.

I look back and see how being the youngest kid gave me a unique perspective. I learned what not to do, like take your parents' or your grandma's cars for a joy ride. Well, at least until you know where all the old stumps are!

## I Love the LucyMobile

I was watching some late-night television the other night. You know the stations that bring you the old shows that you grew up watching? I tuned in just in time to catch an episode of "I Love Lucy." Not just any episode. No, this was the one in which they were heading to California in a 1955 Pontiac convertible. It brought back some memories.

I started to school in 1955 and was looking forward to it with great anticipation. School seemed to be where you went when you were a big kid. Who doesn't want to be a big kid?

Maybe my brother Nick tired of hearing of my constant zeal. I don't know. But my brother started telling me that school wasn't that great. You would have homework and there were mean kids and, worst of all, the teachers could be real witches! This, of course, deflated my spirits. As the summer progressed and September neared, I was rapidly beginning to fear the start of school.

The morning came in late August when I broke into tears at breakfast. Dad consoled me and asked where I got an idea that teachers are witches. It was about this time my brother asked to leave the table, but not until after Dad dealt with him.

Dad tried to undo the damage and decided to take me for a ride. We went to the park and got ice cream cones. We then drove to the school and walked around the building. He showed me the playground with its swings and seesaws and merry-go-round. I began to feel better. Then I saw it!

Sitting next to the back of the building, with its trunk lid up, was a 1955 Pontiac convertible. Suddenly, I felt better! In my six-year-old brain, I knew two things for certain. That was the car Lucy and Desi drove, and Lucy and Desi were not witches. If the Lucy car was at my soon-to-be school, there couldn't be any witches there.

We started to leave the playground and were nearing the two-toned blue Pontiac. I was captivated by its color and wide whitewalls. Even its top was baby blue. A pretty brunette was closing the trunk. She noticed us and smiled. "Hi there, little guy!" she said to me. "Do you go to school here?"

I only shook my head and looked at her and her car- if it was her car. If it was her car and she was a witch, I didn't seem to care. She was pretty! Dad explained to her why we had been there. He told her I was a bit apprehensive about starting school. Mercifully, he did not tell her my stupid brother had scared me.

She bent down and made eye contact with me. "Well, maybe you'll be in my class. I teach first grade." She held out her hand toward me. "My name is Mrs. Weston. What's yours?"

I didn't see any bubbling caldrons or bat wings - and surely witches didn't have cars like that. "Michael," I said, and shook her hand. The ride home found me hoping that she would be my teacher. I asked Dad if what Nick told me was true. He asked me what I thought, to which I said, "No." Dad laughed and said that Nick did pile it on pretty deep.

I hit the kitchen door on the run, looking for my

brother. I found him on the couch reading a comic book. In a move a Ninja would be proud of, I ran toward him, and with all the strength I could muster, kicked him in the shin. Just as quickly, to preserve my life, I turned and fled! I flew past my dad, who stepped between me and Nick. It was sweet listening to the hand of justice deal its comeuppance to my dear brother.

The big day finally arrived, and as luck would have it, I was assigned to Mrs. Weston's class. It was great! We had fun, especially since my best friend, Billy, was in her class too. She had a way of making the most mundane of tasks seem like you were being bestowed a great privilege.

For example, the most obedient, well-behaved student of the week would be assigned to clap the erasers the following week. We older readers know about this, but I will try to explain to the younger among us. Do they still use chalkboards? I don't know. Well, what would happen was the kid who was elected that week's trustee would take the blackboard erasers outback and "clap" them to remove the excess chalk dust. A great honor, whereby the honoree would usually return to the classroom looking like Lot's wife!

One afternoon, I told Billy Mrs. Weston had a wonderful "Lucy Mobile." Of course, he said, "No, she didn't." "Did too," I told him, and I would show him after school. So, when school let out, the two of us took off looking for the car. What we were supposed to do was go catch our school bus! And, of course, we missed our bus. But we did find the lovely Lucy Mobile! We looked in awe and reverently touched it. It had looked like rain that afternoon, and suddenly a flash of lightning streaked through the sky, accompanied by a loud thunderclap!

Billy and I were terrified! There was no one else in

the parking lot. We tried the door, and the Pontiac was open! We got in and closed the door. My friend and I were scared now! A million thoughts ran through our minds. We never considered that our parents would eventually be looking for us. No, we were afraid Mrs. Weston would be mad at us. We eventually agreed that Lucy wouldn't be, but were afraid Mrs. Weston would be upset to find two kids in her car in a rainstorm. We were scared, yet comforted by the warmth of the interior.

We thought it had been forever, sitting in the rain, when it had only been an hour. Mrs. Weston came and got in behind the wheel. She was not terribly surprised to find us in her car. "Do you boys know your parents are very worried about you?" she said in that first grade, sing-song voice. "Fortunately, you were seen getting in my car. I will take you home."

Uh, oh! We had been caught! We're doomed now! Billy and I pleaded with her. Don't leave us! Attempts to persuade her to take us home with her fell on deaf ears. Billy even promised we did not eat much. We would clean her erasers forever! She found that amusing, but wheeled into my parent's driveway anyway. Billy's parents were there also. Like lambs led to the slaughter, Mrs. Weston escorted us in. We were hugged. There was not to be any public flogging!

Mrs. Weston joined our parents for coffee and cake and asked us what was going on. I explained that Billy did not believe that our teacher had a car like Lucy's, so I showed him, and we were caught in the storm and, of course, we apologized. Our parents and Mrs. Weston were not following until Billy explained about her car being like the car on "I Love Lucy." They finally understood what we meant, which prompted our teacher to lecture us about not getting in strange cars.

Mrs. Weston told us she would watch "I Love Lucy" to see her car. The rest of the first grade went well, with our teacher and the LucyMobile. Billy and I never heard it do the babaloo.

*Past the Hood Ornament*

## *The Angel and McFonzie*

In September of 1955, my friend Billy and I only lived six blocks from the school, but for the first few weeks, until we got used to going to school, we rode the bus. Then we walked, like all of the other neighborhood kids.

One afternoon we were leaving school to head home, but were still on school property. We two recently turned six-year-olds were walking across the playground when we were accosted by Edwin and his toady. They were twelve and demanded our change, all thirty-five cents. They then ran off to wait for their bus. We were in tears, standing by the chain link fence.

A shiny, black '40 Pontiac coupe stopped at the curb. The coupe had wide whites and baby moon hubcaps. It had a unique growl, as Colin, the driver, had added to it a split exhaust manifold. It also had fuzzy dice hanging from the rear view mirror.

Rachael "Red" McDowell stepped from the passenger side, walked over to us and squatted down in front of us. Red, her brother Colin, and their father were friends of our family. She was seventeen and a senior at the high school around the corner. Colin was sixteen and a junior.

Their mother had passed away three or four years earlier, and they were like family, and so kind. Red was not quite five feet tall and weighed maybe 95 pounds. She got her nickname from her red hair, of course. Red was Irish and had shamrock green eyes and pale white complexion. Her voice and accent sounded like Roma Downey.

"So, Michael, Billy. Why the tears then?" She reached in her jacket pocket and handed us some tissues.

Between sobs and sniveling, we explained what had happened. She smiled at the two skinny little kids in front of her, turned her head over her shoulder and motioned for Colin.

Colin turned off the coupe and joined his sister. At sixteen, he was close to six feet tall and weighed close to 270 pounds, none of it fat. He was his father's son, who was Daniel "Eric the Red" McDowell. Eric the Red came by the name the same way his daughter did. His hair was red, as was his full beard.

Eric was a weightlifter who came over and worked out with my dad and friends. He was six feet tall and weighed 300 pounds. He gained local notoriety when some guy at one of the pubs hit him. Eric cleared the place and was finishing a Guinness when the police arrived. He had large, powerful hands, as was the rest of him. He was a mill worker with my dad. He drove a '52 Buick Super convertible in red with black top and interior.

Red explained to Colin what had happened to us. She stood up and pointed out the two juvenile delinquents who were waiting for their bus. Colin entered the playground and strode over to where the two miscreants stood. Colin looked like, well, an Irish Fonzie, red hair combed like the Fonz, black leather jacket over a white tee-shirt, jeans and black engineer boots.

"Aaaaah, lads!" No, he didn't say that, but it would have been McCool, though!

## Past the Hood Ornament

Mrs. Adams was on duty, supervising the kids awaiting their buses. Mrs. Adams knew Colin and his family and had taught Red and Colin when they were each fourth graders. She watched the muscle-bound McFonzie walk up to the two boys. Every kid was watching as Colin stopped in front of Edwin and Ben, as they leaned against the fence.

In his Celtic accent, he told Ben, "You, stay where you are." With his right hand, he grabbed Edwin's jacket and picked him up, pushing him against the fence. He named Billy and my names, stating, "You took the lads' money. You will hand it over, won't you?"

Edwin nodded as Mrs. Adams walked up to Colin. Red, Billy and I joined them. Mrs. Adams was told by Red what had happened; all the while Colin held Edwin against the fence.

Finally, Colin spoke. "I'll put you down and you will give them back their money. And if you pick on any other kids, I'll come looking for you. Go ahead and tell your old man. I'll deal with him, too!"

The bully nodded and Colin put him down. Immediately, Edwin emptied his pockets into Colin's hand, who gave it to Red, who gave it to us. Mrs. Adams was lecturing the crowd on bullying and taking what isn't yours as Edwin's bus pulled up.

Billy and I thanked Red and Colin as we left the playground. "Red," I said, "Me and Billy only had thirty-five cents." I handed her the coins and she counted them. "A dollar and fifty-five cents," she said, looking at Colin.

"Well, lads, consider it a bit of interest. If those punks bother you again, let me know. Come on. We'll give you a ride home."

We rode home in the old coupe with its split manifold giving it a raspy growl, though it didn't sound anything like a GTO. We were let out at my place, and since my mom was not home, we went next door to Mrs. Merle's. She gave us a glass of milk and a fresh, homemade cinnamon roll, then poured herself a cup of coffee and joined us.

"Well, boys, how was your day?" She noticed the pile of coins on the table. "What are the coins for?"

We explained to Mrs. Merle what happened with Edwin and how Red and Colin came to the rescue, though neither of us knew what interest was. Mrs. Merle gave us another nickel and divided the money, eighty cents each for me and Billy.

"You know, boys, the Lord was with you today. You know he will send angels to help you when you need it, and I believe that is what happened today." She continued sipping her coffee.

Billy and I looked at each other wide-eyed. "You mean Red's an angel?" Billy asked. We both had a slight problem envisioning Colin as an angel.

"Well, I'll just say the Lord used her as your guardian angel. I didn't say she was literally an angel, boys. God used Red and Colin to help you. Thank Him for your guardian angels. That includes Red and Colin." Then, she laughed! "My word, Colin must have put the fear of the Lord in those boys!"

That evening at dinner I explained what had happened to us and how Red and Colin helped us. My dad leaned back in his chair and looked at me. "You mean, Colin got a hold of the lad?"

I nodded and Nick laughed and commented, "Just what doctors recommend for the heartbreak of constipation!" Mom slapped him on the shoulder. None of them would explain what he meant.

For two weeks, Billy and I followed Red around and waited on her every chance we had, finally asking her if she and Colin were angels.

As Red put it, "No, laddies, I'm no angel. Just a colleen who loves you as my own." She thought it was humorous that we thought so, however.

Red went off to college and became a university history professor who married a minister. Colin did a tour in the Army and then joined the fire department. When I saw him last he had a '69 Catalina sedan, a new bride and a baby on the way. He was still very muscular, though his hair was cut differently.

If I had only asked him about what my brother said.

*life through the rearview mirror*

## Uncle Miltie's On

In the early and mid-'50s, television was still in its infancy. With few exceptions, you did not buy one at a "big box store." You would buy one from quaint, locally owned stores, such as Ed's TV & Appliances.

In our town, the place to get your television was Kelly's Electronics. Milton Kelly had been established as a radio and stereo repairman and dealer when TV came out. He became one of the first dealers in our area to sell them. His shop was on the corner of one of the busiest streets downtown. Mr. Kelly's first name was Milton, and most people called him "Uncle Miltie," after the immensely popular Milton Berle. His shop was filled with televisions, radios and stereos. These stereos were the old, wooden floor models that consisted of a turntable and built-in radio, sometimes a storage place for your records. They, and the period televisions, would usually have polished wood cabinets with a speaker grille covered in fancy fabric.

Uncle Miltie would handle the service calls himself, leaving two sales personnel to watch the store. Uncle Miltie always wore a freshly laundered, white, starched shirt and a bow tie. He was kind of short and a little overweight, with black hair that he slicked back. We kids thought that he was a very nice, jovial man.

It was his service truck that caught your eye, however. He drove a 1954 GMC 1/2 ton pickup which

*Past the Hood Ornament*

was painted white. Kelly's Electronics was painted on the doors, but the bed was the attention getter. He had built a bed cover, sort of like a camper shell, made of wood, and had finished it to look like a television. It was varnished in cherry. The lift gate was made to look like a television screen, complete with painted on knobs. He even had a set of fake rabbit ears on the top! The locals thought it was great, especially us kids. If you were behind it in traffic, you would almost expect to see "Howdy Doody" or "I Love Lucy" on the screen.

One afternoon, our reception was really terrible, so Mom called Uncle Miltie. Shortly before five o'clock, he pulled into our driveway. It was a minor problem - the antennae wire had come loose. Does anyone remember those? Cable and satellite dishes have replaced them. Anyway, Uncle Miltie was not in his truck. He was on his way home and drove his car, a brand-new 1956 Pontiac Safari. My brother and I were taken by this lovely yellow and white sporty wagon. No, he assured us, he was not going to haul televisions in it. Good! We agreed it would be a shame to do that to this car.

It was beautiful. It even had wire wheel covers. Uncle Miltie was married and had two teenagers. He said he was going to buy a replacement sedan, but saw the wagon and had to have it. It was one of the most distinctive cars around, and the people of our fair city thought it was a perfect match for the TV mobile. Well, the Safari did not have fake rabbit ears. I can remember being crazy about the amber Chief on my grandmother's car, though this '56 didn't have one. I liked the "Pontiac" emblem on the wire wheels, however.

The following Monday, Uncle Miltie delivered a new television to our neighbor, Mrs. Merle. Uncle Miltie delivered her new RCA and installed the outdoor antennae. All the while, a small gathering of neighborhood kids surrounded his TV mobile. See, it's not every day a kid can look at a truck that you might be able to watch Captain Kangaroo on!

Uncle Miltie had the most recognizable truck in town, and the one most popular with the kids. (OK, so the ice cream truck may have been a bit more popular). Increased sales grew his business daily. As sales increased, service calls increased. This lead Uncle Miltie to hire another repairman. Of course, Uncle Miltie went to the GMC dealership to find a suitable, used unit, a 1953 half ton. This was painted white with his store's name painted on the doors. And, of course, a matching television was erected over the bed. Take that, competitors! Two TV mobiles were patrolling our city streets! Just more for the kids to go nuts over.

The man Uncle Miltie hired was young and had learned his trade in the military. His name was Harry. He had done a tour in Korea as a radio repairman and two years in the States as a USAF repairman on aircraft radios. He was thin, and to us kids looked a bit like James Dean, or maybe Fonzie. His hair was in a ducktail and though he wore a bow tie and white shirt, a la Uncle Miltie, he was different.

Harry drove a '51 Ford; it was nosed and decked and had fender skirts, along with the dual Smithy's mufflers, something Fonzie might drive. When he was not at Uncle Miltie's, he was behind the wheel of his car, cigarette dangling from his lips.

One day, Uncle Miltie and Harry both had service calls that morning and decided to meet for lunch at Sunni's Cafe. Uncle Miltie had been happy with his new employee's performance. He needed to loosen up a bit, but maybe it was the war in Korea, Miltie thought.

Uncle Miltie paid for the lunch and went to the

store. Harry had a few more service calls to make. It was a hot July afternoon, and Harry stopped before his last call for a bottle of cold beer. He sat in the parking lot of the grocery store, tailgate down, TV screen up. He sat on the GMC's tailgate and enjoyed his beer and smoked a cigarette. He then went to his next call. Nothing serious, just replacing a tube and he was on his way back to the shop.

As Harry entered the business district, only six blocks from Kelly's Electronics, he smelled smoke. He pulled over and jumped out! The back of the GMC was on fire! The wooden TV cover, and the three televisions in the bed were burning! The police and fire trucks arrived, but not before the poor GMC burned up.

Newspaper photographers were there when Uncle Miltie pulled up in his Safari. They said he was livid! What had happened? He approached Harry as the police were questioning him. The police told Uncle Miltie that Harry had stopped for a beer and evidently tossed his match over his shoulder, which caught some shop towels on fire...which caught the broken televisions on fire...which...

The morning paper had a picture of Uncle Miltie belting Harry while the police were pulling him off of his ex-employee. Yes, the Safari could be seen in the background.

I learned years later that Harry left town with a fractured jaw. Uncle Miltie did even a greater business as news of what had happened spread. Our town supported its own, or maybe they had no use for rebels without a cause!

*life through the rearview mirror*

## Salon Chez Debbie

It was glorious summer, August to be exact. We would start the second grade in three weeks and Billy and I were having a great time enjoying our last days of freedom. We were at his parent's house being watched by Billy's sister Debbie and her friend Ellen. They were almost twelve but mature, although, as you read on, you will probably disagree.

We were in the backyard playing war with toy rifles. We were crawling on our bellies in the grass and shooting each other. The back door opened and the two girls stepped out. "Mikey! Come here, sweetie," Debbie said, with as much sweetness as any almost twelve-year-old could.

We both ran to see what they wanted. "Mikey, would you mind being a dear and letting us use you for a model?" Before I could answer, Billy yelled, "No! She's going to make you look like a girl!"

I looked at Billy, not knowing whether to run or not. They didn't look evil.

"Please, Michael," they both implored. "We need your help, and it won't take long. We tried Billy once, but he won't cooperate. Pretty please? We'll give you guys milk and cookies," they pleaded.

"You promise it won't take long, and you promise not to tell, cross your heart?" Billy was doing the negotiating for me, it appeared.

They crossed their collective hearts. Well, okay. It appeared to be a done deal. We went up to Debbie's room. While they were doing what they needed to do, I made Billy swear to me that he would never mention this. We spit shook. That is where you spit in your hand, both parties, and shake. Debbie saw us.

"Ewwww!! What in the world are you doing? You two get in here right now!" She took us across the hall to the bathroom. She made us wash up. Ellen commented, "Ugh! You two smell!"

Okay, I admit we didn't smell exactly like Old Spice. We had been crawling around the backyard. They physically washed our faces and dabbed on some of Mr. Wilmont's aftershave.

Back in Debbie's room, I stood at her window while they readied my torture. We were on the second floor, and to my right, six houses away, was my house. No one was there. I started to fantasize about an escape. You know, like in the old westerns where a cowboy is shot, but gallantly crawls away amid gunfire. If he can only make it to his faithful horse!

This was 1956, and in a few months, Billy's mom would buy a '57 Star Chief convertible. My parents would buy a '57 Oldsmobile Super 88, 4-door hardtop, but at this time I could imagine my jumping out the window like those cowboys did. Of course, I would not have survived, but my imagination had me crawling up the street with a broken leg and in much pain. I would then get into a '56 Star Chief convertible. Our pediatrician had one, a pretty red and white.

"Okay, Mikey. We're ready for you," the girls called in unison, and I was snapped back into reality.

They combed my hair back, even though it was not very long. What they were doing was practicing how to apply makeup.

Every so often, Billy would giggle or snort, which earned him dirty looks from the girls. Debbie put a very small amount of some flesh-colored lotion in the palm of her hand. She dipped her index finger into it, and put a bit at different spots on my face. Both girls were applying this stuff gently with their fingers.

I was seated in Debbie's desk chair, with my back to her dresser mirror. They told me to be still and then they bent down, one on each side of me, and began to dab some blue stuff on my eyelids. Of course, Billy hollered, which brought threats of his expulsion from the room. He calmed down.

I was feeling uneasy about all of this. Billy's snickering didn't help much. I had known Debbie all of my life, and Ellen maybe three years. I guess the good thing was that I learned that I would never be a cross dresser. I did not like having this stuff on my face.

We progressed right along with the girls as they put lipstick on me next. "Go like this," Debbie said and puffed her lips out. When I did this, Billy howled again. Ellen smacked him a good one and Debbie gave him a look that shut him up.

The girls told me to sit still and they put their heads together, all the while keeping an eye on Billy. They decided to take a break. Not me, them. They sent Billy downstairs to get some cookies. At least, a chocolate chip cookie would ease the pain of cruel indignities.

When he returned with the cookies, I was told how to eat them without smearing my lipstick. Oh, the humility! Of course, my good, dear pal broke out laughing. Debbie smacked him this time! Had I been free to get up and leave, I would have. How could he do this to me? Where was my '56 Star Chief getaway car? I felt as though I was being shot or mortally wounded. If I could only make it to the Pontiac!

The girls said I had smeared the lipstick and reapplied it. All the while, Billy was perched on Debbie's bed, biting his lip, at times placing his hand over his mouth. I knew he was laughing. Come on, Star Chief, help me escape all of this!

About the time they were through with me, Ellen picked up a pair of clip-on earrings from Debbie's dresser and clipped them to my earlobes! Billy stood up and came closer, looking over Ellen's shoulder. Once more, he started laughing.

Yeah, Billy was laughing. He had turned and was bent over Debbie's bed. He was laughing and slapping the bed in great gales of hysteria. They were ignoring him and telling me to pay him no attention, when we heard something like the sound of five yards of starched linen being slowly torn asunder. This got their attention!

"You nasty pig!" Debbie cried. She and Ellen began to punch and pound Billy with pillows. I seized the moment! I was free! I turned around and could not believe what was looking back at me in the mirror. I looked like a boy named Sue! Like the kid in "Home Alone." I screamed, and not because of aftershave burn.

They stopped pounding Billy and ran to me. "Michael, hey, take it easy! Calm down! Come here!" They took my hand and drug me to the bathroom across the hall. They scrubbed and scrubbed some more, and after about five minutes, I was makeup and earring free.

The two girls thanked me and said I could go. I don't know who hit the backdoor first, me or Billy. We didn't stop running until we were behind the elm tree in the backyard. We stood there catching our breath and finally I hugged him. "Thanks for what you did! You saved my life."

"Awww, it was nothing. You would have done the

same for me." He looked like a seven-year-old hero. "You would have, wouldn't you?" I told him of course, but was thinking that would depend on whether I had chocolate milk.

"If you hadn't rescued me, they would have had me in saddle shoes and a poodle skirt." It was a thought I shuddered at. We spent the remainder of the afternoon playing war.

Every time I see one of the late-night cowboy movies, I think of this incident. I figure the Star Chief would be an easier rescue. It would be hard to get on the horse if you had been shot or had a broken leg. Yeah, I'll go with the Pontiac!

Uh, has anyone seen my poodle skirt?

## Elves, Hearses, and Rainbows Over the Hills

It looked like a scene from a Currier & Ives painting. Winter, of course. Snow everywhere. Kids bundled up in snowsuits and high top black galoshes. Mittens and mufflers of every conceivable color. Ear muffs or caps with pull down, fur lined ear and neck warmers. Kids were king of the hill. This was Quarter Mile Hill.

No, it didn't say that on the street sign, but standing at the top looking down, well, it was about a quarter of a mile down the steepest hill in town. It belonged to the kids until the spring thaw. The residents of the street couldn't climb it until spring, so it was blocked off and used as a sled run.

At the top, to your left, was a Sinclair gas station. To your right was the Chevrolet-Oldsmobile dealership. Looking straight ahead you would see the courthouse and municipal buildings. Fifty feet from the street, the hill began its descent. It was at that point that the city had erected the barricades, allowing access to the station and dealership.

Looking back, that second week in December of 1957 was beautiful. Snow, Christmas lights and decorations on houses. The smell of coal and wood being burned. And kids! It seemed every kid in the county was on that hill that afternoon. It was below freezing beneath the gray afternoon sky. The air was filled with the sound of children's laughter and shrieks, and remnants of frozen breath.

At the bottom of the hill was a two-way residential street which had been barricaded a block in either direction. Had you turned left or right, you would have wound up in a small park between the high school and elementary school.

It was on this hill the previous winter, while riding tandem with Billy, that we fell off the sled after hitting a bump. We slid almost a quarter of a mile on the seat of our pants. That afternoon, one of the greatest scientific discoveries was made. Not frostbite. No, frost butt! How can anything that cold burn?

As if the hill didn't attract enough kids, the courthouse square had erected a Santa Village. Well, maybe not a village. It was a wooden shed decorated in Christmas gaiety. Santa was in there. Bring the kids to see him. Have a picture made, and see the elves!

Ah, yes! The elves! Billy and I were eight at the time, but we noticed that Santa on the town square had more guys bringing runny-nosed kids than the department store Santas. The department stores seemed to be full of housewives, mothers. Not the town square! No, these lines were full of mill workers, mechanics, working class stiffs with a couple of kids in tow.

One day, Billy got my attention and said, "Hey, Mike, Nick's over there!" My big brother. Yeah, there he was. He and his best friend Gary. They were fifteen and reminded us of Wally Cleaver and Eddie Haskell. (You figure out which). So we ran over to see what they were doing.

"Nick! What are you guys here for?" I asked. He shook his head and looked at Gary, then at me and Billy. "What do you think, twerp?" Suddenly, I was talking to

## Past the Hood Ornament

two Eddie Haskells. "The elves. The elves, stupid!" Billy and I shrugged and looked around. There were lots of high school boys around. Then we got it! Elves! Actually, high school girls in Christmas elf costumes. Santa had eight or ten of them. They wore little pixie hats, curly-toed elf shoes and green elf jackets over little, dinky green skirts! Aha! Mystery solved!

The Sears Santa didn't have young, teenage girls' legs on display! It didn't last very long, however. The local housewives and church ladies put the elves out of business. It was the high school boys, mill workers, and mechanics who wanted to see the cute elves' legs! How many times can you drag your kid to see Santa anyway?

Back to the hill. We were officially out on Christmas break and spirits were high. (Well, except those that would miss the elves. The mayor had spoken. Next year, there would be no teenage girl elves. The mayor's wife had spoken also!)

It was cold that afternoon, bitterly cold. People scurried about town doing last-minute shopping. Christmas carols drifted from the Chevrolet dealership. There were not as many kids out that day. Some had gone to relatives for the holiday. This was a good thing, as you will see in a minute.

It had begun to snow again as Billy, several other boys and I stood next to a 55-gallon drum with a fire in it. Officer McMinn, a city policeman, was there too, having been assigned to watch the hill. We watched the '53 Pontiac hearse - yes, hearse - pull onto our street. It quickly turned onto the Sinclair station's property.

We kids thought that hearse was creepy. It was big and very shiny black. It had wide whitewalls and the big glass side window with dark velvet curtains. Scary! So was its driver, Mr. Timmons. He parked right next to the street, aiming down the hill.

Mr. Timmons stepped out, leaving the hearse's engine idling, its left wheels on the street. All we kids knew about him was that he drove that hearse. Pontiac or not, we hated it! It looked like something Dracula would drive. It didn't help that he was tall, thin...and, why do undertakers have to look like extras in slasher movies?

He yelled to Officer McMinn that he was getting cigarettes and went into the station. Meanwhile, we boys stared at the idling hearse. We watched its exhaust rise in the cold air.

What was that noise? A thump came from the Pontiac. It started moving! Billy and I and the other boys were terrified! It began to move a bit faster, rolling down the hill. Mr. Timmons was running across the station drive. He slipped and fell on the street.

Officer McMinn blew his whistle and screamed at the kids on the hill on sleds. He tried to reach the runaway hearse, but slipped and fell. Have you ever tried to run on ice?

The Pontiac hearse easily nudged the barricades aside and was gaining speed. A crowd filled the street between the Sinclair station and the dealership. They had heard the screams and whistle. We boys jumped into the front yard of the house behind us as the hearse (from hell) hit the drum, spewing fire in its wake. Fortunately, snow and ice do not burn!

It was now rapidly heading downhill. Amid a sea of terrified kids, many with freshly wet pants, the hearse raced by. Unbelievable! It hit the street at speed, hit the curb on the other side and became airborne. Airborne! It was off the ground as it took out a park bench and crashed to the ground!

It was mayhem - kids crying, whimpering, parents embracing their children. Officer McMinn was red in the face. "You! I don't know the charges, but you are under arrest!" Mr. Timmons did not argue. The citizens were irate. I expected to hear, "Get a rope!" They always said that in Roy Rogers' movies.

By the time we got to the bottom of the hill, an Autocar diesel was retrieving the hearse. To this day, I do not know - don't want to know - if the old Pontiac had an occupant. As we neared our houses, Billy asked me in hushed tones, "Did...did you wet your pants?"

In retrospect, I think Quarter Mile Hill had a rainbow over it that afternoon!

## Reading Is Fundamental

It had been a very good summer so far, and it was only beginning. My best friend Billy and I had just turned eleven, he in May and I in June. As was our routine on Saturdays, we would go to the park for a baseball game. Well, Billy liked to play. I went to - what does the song say? Root, root, root for the home team.

We were hot and dusty this afternoon and in good spirits. The home team had indeed won. Usually after a game we would get a Coke and walk to the library. We were both avid readers, and for the past six months or so had been into *Ivanhoe*, *The Three Musketeers* or anything Arthurian. Yeah, I know, but at least we didn't have to be told to read.

The library was close to downtown on a two-lane street lined with trees and park benches. Those benches gave a spectacular view of the river. The library itself was a large turn of the century, red brick building. It had that wonderful, old book aroma that made you want to pour a glass of milk, get a cookie, and curl up with one of its volumes.

There was a young librarian, no more than 25 at most, who had joined the staff two years ago. Billy and I thought she looked like Debbie Reynolds. Her name was Miss Colby, and she always greeted us with a big smile, even if we had just come from a baseball game. Do you remember how sweaty, dusty, and smelly kids can get? Either she was extremely nice or she had sinus trouble.

As we were checking out our books with Miss Colby, she asked us if we would be interested in helping out at the upcoming book sale. We had no idea what she meant. She explained that in two weeks the library was going to sell some old books. They would set up a booth and tables in the back parking lot. It didn't pay anything, but she would bring us lunch.

Man! We were thrilled! Surely, it must be because we were such studious young men, patrons who appreciated great literature. Howbeit, we were a bit aromatic at the moment. We were told that a high school girl would be helping, and all we had to do was run messages between her and the library itself. This was before cell phones, text and iPods, you must remember.

We assured her that we would. Billy even said he would give up his ballgame to do this. I promised her that we would not stink. Miss Colby laughed. Billy kicked me in the shin! He told me as we carried our books home that he liked her, and that I had said a very stupid thing. Well, he forgave me.

Billy asked me if I knew what kind of car Miss Colby had. No, I didn't, and I thought Billy must be in love. Why else would he ask such a thing? Actually, he didn't know. He knew I was better at telling one car from another. He said he had not gotten close enough to tell what it was. He described it as being two-toned. The top, and a part on the side, was a not dark, not light green. The rest of it was a yellow-green. It had two doors. On the side was a chrome-looking light, and the taillights had two round lenses on each side. It had whitewall tires and four headlights. Oh, yeah, and a big grill. Now, I'm thinking, "Billy, you want me to tell you what kind of car it is from that description?"

We had made it to the park and were about to turn onto our street when a horn blew behind us. We looked over our shoulders as Miss Colby waved and drove by. It was beautiful! What a color! "Geez, Billy," I said. "That's a '58 Bonneville." Billy sighed. "Yeah, beautiful, isn't she?"

I didn't know if he meant the car or Miss Colby. Come to think of it, he would have been right on either. My friend was in love with an older woman, and her would-be suitor didn't use deodorant yet that I knew of. My good friend, I feared, would be hurt, scarred for life by a broken heart. I knew these things. I was the only kid I was aware of who read Shakespeare for enjoyment. Alas! Poor Billy. I knew him well! The tempestuous pains of unrequited love!

The next day he came over, and I must say, we both smelled much better. It had begun to rain, so we spent the afternoon reading Hamlet. Billy thought the soliloquy was funny. That's okay. I find algebra a bit humorous. Let's see, I have five dollars and I'm going to subtract XY to the third power, and if the train leaves Chicago at 5:45, how many apples does Betty have left? Billy was a gifted mathematician.

The following Saturday, Billy's team won again. The team was happy until he announced that he was sitting out the next game. There was no joy in Mudville when the kids found out the reason for his absence. One kid got in his face and said they would lose without him. Billy shrugged his shoulders, and the other boy hit Billy. Not a smart move. As my neighbor lady, Mrs. Merle, once said, "There comes a time to smite the Philistines." Well, the time arrived. Billy hit the kid in his mouth, and a couple of other team members started after my friend.

I had been told by my brother if you ever get in a fight with more than one guy, go for the biggest one first. I headed toward the biggest kid I saw with a clenched fist, but I didn't hit him. I kicked him as hard as I could in the groin, then hit the boy beside him in the face. By this time, Billy had picked up a baseball bat and was waving it and saying he would fight them one at a time. Good old Billy. I was heavier, but Billy didn't run. As they left, Billy told them what they could do with their team.

The bruises were gone by the time of the book sale. We arrived fresh and odor-free. Miss Colby's Bonneville could be seen over in the staff parking area. Just as the sale was beginning, a '54 red Pontiac convertible, top down, pulled up beside Miss Colby's car. A tall young man got out. I recognized him as Mr. Stein, a new teacher at the high school.

Billy was already keeping his eye on Miss Colby, but suggested we watch Mr. Stein, who was in the booth helping Miss Colby. Billy and I stayed busy running back and forth delivering messages. We had been speaking to each other in Elizabethan English. Why? We had been reading so many Arthurian tales of knights. We were just amusing ourselves and having fun.

Miss Colby called us into the booth and told us to eat lunch. We sat on stools in the corner and devoured the sandwiches, chips and soft drinks. We were sitting there, laughing and having a good time. There were no customers at the booth. The high school student was straightening up the tables in the lot.

Billy and I saw them at the same time, over in the far corner in the shadows. Miss Colby and Mr. Stein were kissing! We stood to our feet! The knight mindset kicked in. We must defend her honor! In my best Burtonesque voice I cried, "Knave! Most unworthy wretch! Dare thee besmirch the lady's honor? Explain thyself!"

Startled, they broke their embrace and faced us. Billy picked up the gauntlet. "Stain the good lady's name? Then make haste to stain the ground with thy blood!" I thought, Well said, my friend!

Without missing a beat, Miss Colby turned and clasped her hands to her breast. "Oh, most noble sirs! I beseech thee, spare the life of the gentleman. I implore thy bounteous mercy, sirs. For 'tis this good man I have pledged my heart. I am his betrothed, and may God speed the day." Oh, well done!

We both applauded her! She curtsied. Had anyone outside the booth heard this? Well!

Several hours later we walked home. "So, Mike, I can't figure it. We're the knights, the good guys. And the knave kisses the lady...and she likes it!" He had a point. Plus, the gorgeous lady had an equally fine Pontiac. The knave's convertible was impressive, too!

I raised my left arm as if holding a sword. "Well, good lords all! One for all, and all for one!"

## Big Red's Produce

He was a fixture around town, Mr. Hertz, driving his '41 GMC 5-ton stake bed. I thought it was attractive, shiny red with black fenders. The gold lettering on the doors proclaimed "Big Red's Produce."

Mr. Hertz was fifty, give or take a few years. He was medium height with red hair and was stout from working his farm, which was located across the river. Red's farm kept the local restaurants, farmer's market and schools supplied with fresh vegetables and apples. He had a large apple orchard.

In the fall, he also produced pumpkins. Big Red grew corn, and I am not sure what else was raised on his place, but the GMC would regularly make trips to town with produce. Crates of produce would be stacked to the top of the stakes and covered with a tarp.

When not bringing his crops to town, Mr. Hertz could be seen behind the wheel of his '48 Pontiac convertible. It too was red with a black top. He also had a new '61 GMC 4-wheel drive. (Of course, it was red).

Mr. Hertz was a kind, jovial man who liked kids. Maybe he regretted not having any of his own, as he had never married. So, every fall he would have a hayride and a corn field maze, apple bobbing booths, pumpkin carvings, and hot apple cider on his farm. Church ladies would bring fresh cookies and pies. Mr. Hertz would charge admission per car, with the proceeds being donated to the local children's home.

The event was very popular with the local kids, who were very fond of Mr. Hertz. Children's home kids looked forward to the event, and it was through the hayride that Mr. Hertz met Miss Olsen. Miss Olsen was a social worker with the children's home. The two had been seeing each other for a year.

My friend, Billy, and I had noticed this. Of course, everyone else in town did too. You know what they say about news (gossip is what it is) traveling fast. Well, Billy and I at first wondered what Winesap thought, but decided he must like Miss Olsen. Oh, Winesap was Big Red's German Shepherd who rode with him on his deliveries. Winesap was popular with the kids, too. A neat name, don't you think?

Mr. Hertz and Winesap were making a delivery to our school one afternoon when I noticed Winesap was limping slightly. I got down on my knees to inspect his paw. A teacher asked me what I was doing. Actually, she told me to leave the dog alone. She didn't want to hear that he had a pebble between his toes. I pulled it out. Winesap licked me. The teacher sent me to the office. Today, Winesap would not be allowed near the school, which probably would be in the best interest of the dog.

October brought chilly weather, changing leaves and flyers on the school bulletin board about the approaching Hertz Farm hayride and maze event. Shortly after the school year started, Billy won the heart of one of the little girls from the children's home. No, no, no, not like that. Besides, we were only twelve.

Billy came to the rescue of a girl one afternoon. Kids being kids, sometimes the kids from the children's home were picked on. Why? Because they were orphans. Go figure! We were at recess and a boy from our class was over by the swings, teasing a seven-year-old girl.

Her offense? She was an orphan. The girl was almost in tears when Billy caught what was going on. Billy walked over and got between the girl and our classmate.

"You got a problem, Nate? What'd she do to you, huh? You got nothing better to do than pick on little girls?" Billy then called him a choice name and belted him upside his head, which sent him to the ground.

This drew a crowd of kids, and a teacher who asked the usual questions. Billy was furious, so angry he was oblivious to the teacher. He told Nate that if he bothered her, or any kid from the home, he would have to deal with him! When the teacher learned what had happened, she sent Nate to the office and thanked Billy for standing up to bullies.

The little girl was named Leslie. She tugged at Billy's sleeve and thanked him. Every chance she had, she would be close to him. Nate, on the other hand, kept his mouth shut and stayed away from Billy.

My friend and I were walking home that mid-October Friday afternoon. Mr. Hertz and Miss Olsen had just passed by and waved. We had made it down to the park when another horn blew, and a '56 Buick sedan full of teenagers pulled up to the curb.

Deborah, Billy's sister, got out and waved bye to the other girls. If you remember, it wasn't that long ago that Debbie – or Deborah as she was calling herself now – had practiced her make up application techniques on me. Deborah was seventeen now, and a senior who would graduate in May. I would never tell her so, but she was pretty– blond hair, blue eyes and dimples when she smiled. She planned to become a doctor.

"Hey, guys, we need to talk." she said, motioning to a park bench. She considered me as her other brother. She was like a big sister to me. "First, not a word of this, or I'll throttle you. Got it?" she said sternly. We nodded.

"You don't know what you started when you beat up that kid, do you?"

Before he could answer, she went on. "Mom and Dad have talked to me. So, little brother, how would you like to have a little sister?"

"What? Are you crazy? A baby sister?" He looked at me in bewilderment. I could only shrug.

"No, dummy!" Deborah said. "Not a baby. Look, I'll be gone next fall, and since you protected that little girl, well, they went to the home to see her. They may adopt her. What do you think?"

"You mean Leslie?" Billy smiled. "That would be neat. She's cool. Wait a minute. How did they know who she was?"

"All they had to do was ask. The whole school knows she follows you around, dummy."

Billy smiled again. "That would be cool. She's like you. I mean, if you were seven."

Deborah laughed. "That's what they said. I'll meet her at the hayride. Don't say anything!"

Wow! My friend was like a knight who rescued the fair damsel. It took some getting used to. Billy may have Leslie as his sister.

My dad was at work the day of the hayride, and my Mom was doing something with our neighbor Mrs. Merle, so I rode with Billy's family, the Wilmonts. (Yes, in that lovely '60 Bonneville convertible). It was a beautiful Saturday and Mr. Hertz had plenty of kids turn out. The hayride was a large trailer full of hay (of course), hooked to Mr. Hertz's tractor. The ride was operated every thirty minutes.

The '48 Pontiac was in the driveway in front of the garage. Mr. Hertz had picked up Miss Olsen early that morning. Winesap was trotting along with me and Billy and having a good time. Billy called Leslie over to meet the dog, and she broke away from his parents and sister. As she got closer, she stopped at the sight of the German Shepherd. So, the little blond girl was afraid of dogs.

I dropped to my knees beside Winesap and assured Leslie that the dog wouldn't hurt her. Billy did the same thing. We told Winesap to sit. "Look, Leslie," I said. "His name is Winesap, like the apple. He'll shake hands. See?" I held out my hand, and the Shepherd placed a paw in my hand.

Leslie laughed and came closer as Billy assured her. She shook the dog's paw, petted him, and worked up the courage to hug him. She received a lick in response. Leslie removed her cardigan, left it with Billy and ran back to his parents.

It was a bit after three when panic erupted. They could not find Leslie. People were calling her name and searching for her. Mr. and Mrs. Wilmont were frantic! Billy still had the sweater, and we decided to let Winesap find her. I mean, he was a dog, right? We let him sniff the sweater and told him to fetch. We had no idea if he would try, or even had an idea what it was we wanted him to do.

He whined a bit, barked, and eventually took off with the two of us right behind. The dog led us to the '48 Pontiac, where he stood and barked. Leslie had gotten in and was asleep on the front seat. It seems she liked the old '48 and had gotten in when she was tired. So Billy's new sister had good taste!

What a day! Winesap was a hero and got a treat. Billy was getting a new sister. And Big Red was getting married! He and Miss Olsen announced their engagement. All in all, it was a fine time for a ride in an old Pontiac, which is what Mr. Hertz did. He put the top down and took Miss Olsen, his soon-to-be wife, Leslie, and her new family, on a lovely afternoon ride!

*Past the Hood Ornament*

## *The Plumbers Friend*

The tranquility of our neighborhood was disrupted in October '63 for eight or nine months. The elderly gentleman who had lived in a once neat house had been placed in a nursing home. The man's son, who lived in New York, hired a management company to rent the house out for him. It was a typical house for our area - a white two-story, with green shutters and a picket-fenced lawn.

Then came Mr. Petrovski.

Mr. Petrovski was a short, balding man in his fifties, with a protruding stomach. My dad said it was a beer belly. We found out that he did indeed like to drink. I wondered why he had rented the large house, as he was alone. The house had four bedrooms, and Mr. Petrovski had never been married. No children. As I said, he lived alone in that big house.

It is important to note that the house was on the opposite side of the street from us, and seven houses up. The street was on an incline before Mr. Petrovski's house, which meant...well, you will see a little later.

The man was a plumber by trade and drove a green 1960 GMC with the company name lettered on the doors. He owned a 1951 Ford sedan that was kept in the driveway in front of the garage. Mr. Petrovski generally drove the truck.

One early November Saturday afternoon, we

noticed the GMC was half on the driveway. The front end was on the lawn. No big deal, right? It would not have been, had it not been obvious that Mr. Petrovski had driven through the picket fence! When the snow came, it covered the broken-down section of fence, and a shirt and countless beer bottles. Evidence of Mr. Petrovski's drinking were mounting. Sometimes they rolled.

Since he lived on the beginning of a hill, sometimes those of us downhill would find beer bottles in the street - literally, though they would tend to be in the gutter. The residents on our block were beginning to complain, especially Mrs. Merle.

Mrs. Merle lived next door on our right. She was very close to (if not already) seventy, with grey hair worn in a bun, and glasses, and she was a bit overweight. She was the stereotypical little old lady. Billy, my best friend, and I loved her. Oh, one other thing: she was a full-gospel, fundamentalist Christian.

One day during Christmas break, Billy and I were on the sidewalk approaching my parent's house. We stopped in our tracks. It was very cold and the snow was deep. Yet, in front of Mrs. Merle's house, standing in the street, were Mrs. Merle and her prayer group. Four more old ladies. They were all buttoned up in winter gear, including hats, boots and gloves. Their heads were tilted back, arms raised. You could see their breath.

Billy punched my arm. "You know, man, I think they are exorcising Mr. Petrovski. You know, to get him out of the neighborhood."

I looked at him and agreed. "Yeah. I guess Mrs. Merle found another Pabst bottle." My friend laughed. "He doesn't know it, but he's doomed."

I knew he was right. Within the week, she had

called the police about the problem. No one could figure why the bottles kept getting in the street, including the police. Mr. Petrovski was ticketed for littering and told that the return of the bottles would mean his lock up.

Things were better after this. If all it took was a call to the police, well, then the neighborhood would do that at the sight of one more beer bottle.

In the meantime, spring was arriving. The snows were gone, replaced with green grass, flowers, and the sound of lawn mowers. Ahhh, good old spring. Well, I guess me being me, I had noticed something new in our city. The police department's cars were 1962-63 Fords, but, over the winter two new '64 models joined the force. Only these two were Pontiacs - black and white, gumball and dog dish caps. I had heard rumors the 389s had a trio of 2-barrel carburetors, Pontiac called it "Tri-Power," and their most powerful engines all had them. Once in a while one would cruise through the neighborhood. They made a lovely burble, whatever the induction system.

Meanwhile, up the street at Mr. Petrovski's house, things looked pretty shabby. A large portion of the picket fence was knocked down. Now it was becoming overtaken by the uncut grass. That old shirt was still where it had been since November. It was now partially hidden by grass and a few of those Pabst bottles. That old Ford had not been driven in a while, and now had a couple of flat tires. The plumbing truck had picked up a couple of dents over the winter.

The neighborhood was disgusted and had begun to complain to the slovenly Mr. Petrovski, particularly the Bennedettos, who lived next door. The couple had two little girls, ten and seven, and were constantly asking Mr. Petrovski to clean up the mess. Yet, he did nothing.

The talk around our street continued. My parents and Billy's said he was a drunk. Others claimed he was crazy. Mrs. Merle said he needed a good "devil chasing dose of the Lord." And who is to say all three opinions weren't right?

Then came the fateful Sunday afternoon in May that became known on our block as the day my dad, my old man, drove the snakes out! The day was beautiful. Perfect weather. Birds in the sky, bees buzzing in the flowers. A few lawn mowers could be heard mingled among the laughter of children playing. Billy and I were sitting on the lawn, talking and watching my dad. He was waxing the recently purchased '64 Catalina. He would not trust me to do it yet, as it was still so new. Our moms were next door, helping Mrs. Merle with her flower garden.

Dad had stopped wiping the trunk lid and wiped his face with his shirt tail. He stopped with his back to the car and gazed at the street. Something was slowly rolling down the street. It clearly wasn't a beer bottle. Whatever it was stopped in front of the driveway. It was a plunger, a plumber's friend! Billy and I looked at each other and panicked. We knew this was not going to be pleasant. Dad was tired of the slob up the street. Slowly Dad looked up the street. There, in all of his bestomached glory was Mr. Petrovski, standing at the tailgate of the truck. He wore no shirt and appeared to be searching the truck bed for something.

My dad picked up the plunger and held it in his right hand. He then turned toward the Petrovski residence, and at the top of his voice began to yell.

"Hey, you fat drunken ..." We will censor the rest in the interest of our younger readers, although I will say that not all of the comment was in English. His parents, my grandparents, were Scottish immigrants. They spoke Scots Gaelic in private, and when Dad was really mad, he would switch back and forth.

Anyway, the block became quiet. People stopped what they were doing to observe. Mrs. Merle and our moms stood behind us watching, my mom trying to calm my dad down. He would have no part of it.

Finally, Mr. Petrovski yelled back not a very nice reply. I will add his speech was very slurred. Oh, yeah, Dad lifted weights for fun and had participated in a few Highland games. So what he did next fit into that. He extended his left arm, turned to the right as far as he could, and snapped back around. The plunger flew straight as an arrow, missing Mr. Petrovski's head by inches. This caused him to extend a hand of friendship toward my father. Actually, it was an upturned middle finger.

Dad took off up the street, my mom yelling at him. Billy and I, now on our feet, couldn't believe this. Billy turned and said to Mrs. Merle, "I guess this is where the Philistine gets smote."

Mr. Petrovski swung at Dad, missed, and fell face down on the street, passed out. Dad grabbed him by his belt and drug him into the front yard.

Officer Royce arrived in his Catalina, siren wailing, and 389 rumbling. The officer found the street crowded with cheering neighbors, except for Mrs. Merle. She had her hands up, praying. Petrovski was arrested, still unconscious, road rash and all. He was evicted within thirty days.

As my friend and I later told Mrs. Merle, "Philistine smitten!"

## XY Squared Over WD 40

Miss Holcomb was a new teacher at our school the year I entered eighth grade. First thing every morning would find me in her Introduction to Algebra class. I can balance my checkbook; otherwise, math and I do not get along. Miss Holcomb did not help any.

Not for the reason you may think. See, she moved to our town right out of college. She was only ten or twelve years older than her students; plus, she was cute. I thought she resembled Judy Garland, and I didn't want to get caught speechless if she called on me.

I sat next to Billy, still my best friend. We studied together. He helped me with math and I helped him with English. In class, though, he would fall on every word (and number) while I was in a fog. I had enough trouble with math, let alone trying to follow Judy Garland explaining how to square X.

I knew Miss Holcomb had a funny little car, one that I could see Judy Garland driving. She drove a 1954 Nash Metropolitan. I had seen a couple on the streets before, but had never known anyone who owned one. It brought to mind a kid's pedal car. It was some sort of shade of pink and white. Barbie would have loved it!

So, I sat in Miss Holcomb's class one morning watching her write an equation on the blackboard: X + Y squared over WD40, divided by the total area of a right angle triangle. Huh?

## Past the Hood Ornament

Miss Holcomb turned and faced us, still holding the chalk. She raised her right hand and pointed at me. "Mike, would you please tell us the value of the divisor?"

No, no, no! I'm caught in the headlights! What is the divisor? WD40? How do you divide something by WD40? God, I could use a little help here! I had no idea. Had she asked me about the conjugation of verbs, or shall I compare her to a summer's rose, I could have answered.

After what seemed like an eternity, she pointed to Billy. He, of course, answered it correctly. Fine! This is just what I needed. Abstract math! I had been doing my best until then to figure the speed of the train which left Baltimore if Sally had four apples and John had a lovely bunch of coconuts! Thankfully, Miss Holcomb was a nice person who would work with you as long as you tried. I did well to maintain a C average, barely.

One frigid early November afternoon, Billy and I were walking home as usual. We had only started and were still in the teachers' parking lot. As we neared Miss Holcomb's Metropolitan, we noticed someone beside it - a fellow member of our math class, David Berg. He was our circle's version of Eddie Haskell. He was on his knees in front of the left rear wheel, screwdriver in hand. The front wheel was missing its hubcap. It was on the ground beside him.

"Berg! What are you doing? Put them back, man!"

I looked around the lot. Not a teacher in sight. He looked up at me, Eddie Haskell-ish. "You going to make me?" he asked.

Before I could answer, Billy stepped forward and told him, "If he doesn't, I will!" Billy couldn't stand young Master Berg. It went back to the year before. My friend liked a girl named Gloria. We were by our lockers one morning and Billy saw her across and down the hall by her locker.

"Mike, Mike, there she is! Give me something to tell her how pretty she is this morning!" he begged. Well, I told him to tell the cute blond girl something to the effect of how her radiance that morning would put the very sun to shame. Billy nodded and trotted off in the direction of Gloria.

The problem came from Berg. His locker was only a few away from Gloria. Berg heard what Billy told Gloria. He thought it was hilarious and started laughing.

I looked in the direction of the laughter in time to see Berg being grabbed by the collar and belted upside his head a couple of times. It shut Berg up, but drew the attention of fellow students and teachers. I don't know if it was because of my words or because Gloria liked manly-type guys, but she and Billy became friends until her family moved to St. Louis.

Maybe it was because Berg had tangled with Billy before, or maybe because most Eddie Haskell types back down when pushed back. Our young miscreant said nothing and reinstalled the rear hubcap. While reinstalling the front, he stopped to ask, "You guys aren't going to rat on me, are you?"

Miss Holcomb walked up before we could answer. "What are you kids doing?"

"We were walking by and Berg noticed your hubcap was loose. He's just making sure it's on."

We found out that the reason Berg was taking the wheel covers was revenge. It seems he was angry over failing a test. I think Miss Holcomb knew we were feeding her a line, though she never said anything. Well, she did thank Berg.

Suspicious or not, that was Miss Holcomb's way. She would give you the benefit of the doubt as long as you tried. Maybe Berg knew that she knew what the real story was. He did a lot better in math after that incident. For a while anyway.

We did our mid-term exams shortly before Christmas break. Despite his efforts, David Berg failed miserably and, of course, he was very upset. His attitude became defiant and he was sent to the office on several occasions. The eighth grade was traditional. We had our homeroom teacher, who handled all of our subjects except math and physical education. Math was the only time I ever saw David Berg. I only knew that after mid-term exams, he changed for the worse. All of the kids noticed it. Billy and I even went so far as to watch the pink and white Metropolitan's hubcaps. Actually, most of the kids watched it, as Berg had a reputation.

It all came to a head toward the end of January. Something pushed him over the edge. Somehow, he had gotten her car keys. It was later determined he had picked them up from her desk. From this point, it was on its way to the fan.

Around lunchtime, Berg drove away from the school in the Barbie mobile. The streets were icy; there was snow on the ground, and it was snowing. Now, a pink and white Metropolitan with a 14-year-old kid behind the wheel is bound to draw attention. I was surprised that he could shift the Metropolitan.

After going through a red light, a city police car fell in behind him. I would say there was a high speed chase but we are talking about a Nash Metropolitan, after all. It was a sixteen mile chase involving two police cars. It came to an end eleven miles outside the city when Berg slid off the road in a curve. The Nash came to rest on its left side in a ditch. David Berg was unhurt, though he was lucky that he was not killed. It had rolled once and only had the convertible top.

Berg was cuffed and taken away. He was expelled and six months later sent to reform school. They were more strict in those days. Today, he would be on "Maury" or "Dr. Phil".

Miss Holcomb took the insurance check and went car shopping. She did her shopping at the Pontiac dealer, of course. Her students were unaware that she had met and began dating the used car sales manager shortly after arriving in our fair city. She purchased a '63 LeMans convertible. It was great, and her students gave her their approval. It was a year old, with low mileage, red with red interior and black top - a very pretty car. It had a 326 and automatic. Much better than the Nash!

Miss Holcomb became a faithful Pontiac customer, eventually marrying the used car sales manager. We students continued to watch the LeMans for her but, after fifty years, I still don't know how to divide WD 40 into XY squared.

*Past the Hood Ornament*

# SECOND GEAR

## Pretty in Pink

Gray's Magic Creations was the place for those with a sweet tooth in our town. It had started as a bakery in the '30s by Mr. Gray's father. It had opened downtown near the courthouse, doing a thriving business serving coffee and donuts. Over the years, it had grown and now occupied a building in a shopping center near subdivisions. The Grays liked the new location in a center with a super market, a hair salon and various clothing stores.

The store itself had changed little in appearance and format. Entering the doors was like stepping back in time to an old-fashioned ice cream parlor. There was a player piano, checkered tablecloths and the most wonderful ice cream shakes, sundaes and banana splits. Helium balloons were given to the children.

The other part of Gray's was the bakery. It was a full-service bakery, with everything from donuts to wedding cakes. Oh, I almost forgot. The ice cream parlor also sold candy - jelly beans, jaw breakers and even gourmet chocolates.

Silas Gray, the owner's son, was a junior at our school. He worked part-time at the shop after school and sometimes on the weekends. He was a tall, gangly, studious individual who was on both the debate and track teams.

Silas had recently begun dating Paula, a cute, fellow member of the debate team, and he found himself looking for a car, As long as it was reliable and was in his slim price range, he didn't care what it was. On his way home from track practice one afternoon, he stopped at Wyatt's Super Service for a Coke. I was washing the station tow truck. I got to talking to Silas for a few minutes. He was telling me about the upcoming track meet when he saw it.

Wyatt was selling a '50 GMC half ton for a friend. Wyatt knew the truck was in great mechanical shape, as he had been the one servicing it. The truck had a very nice interior. The exterior, well, it needed a paint job. It had been painted several times in its life. One of those previous paintings had been white. The last painting was red,only whoever sprayed it did not prep it. No sanding, no primer, just sprayed it over the white.

During the time since the red had been applied, it had faded terribly and now was a dull pink. In certain areas, the white could be seen. None of this mattered to Silas. No. All he needed was reliable transportation. He was confident Paula would not mind riding in a pink truck.

Wyatt said the asking price was $200 (this was 1965!), and Silas and he took it on a test drive. Silas was impressed with how smooth it ran and said if it was all right with his parents, he would take it. They returned the following afternoon, and despite his mother's claim of it being "the ugliest thing on wheels," it now belonged to Silas. His mother would later come to view it in a much different light.

Silas drove to the sweet shop for work after purchasing it. Gray's Magic Creations was a stand alone building in the shopping center. It sat out by the highway and could be readily seen from the other shops. The sight of the pink GMC drew immediate attention. Nearly all of the customers commented or asked about it. People had seen it from the highway and came in for a cup of coffee. Why was it pink? Who had come up with the idea? Questions flew about the old truck. Silas began giving the kids pink balloons. After all, kids liked the colorful pickup!

When Silas wheeled into the student parking lot Monday morning, all eyes were on the GMC. Paula was with him. She was no shrinking violet, a fact testified to by her being on the debate team. She and Silas answered a lot of questions about the paint job. Most of the kids thought it had been painted pink. It was hard to tell differently unless you looked at the spots on the tailgate or cowl, where the white was showing.

Silas took some kidding from the guys over the color. As the weeks went by, the other members of the track team began calling him, you guessed it, Pinky! This didn't bother him much; well, the part that was strange was...Pinky Gray? He considered it part of driving a pink vehicle. He had begun to save for a professional paint job, though he wasn't sure what color he would choose.

The GMC's paint would have to wait for a while. The debate team, including Paula, would be away for a few days. And the track team was also keeping Silas busy. Silas was fast and had helped our school rack up trophies. Some had taken to calling him "The Pink Streak."

At Magic Creations, sales were way up. It seems that it became known as the sweet shop with the pink truck. Suddenly, Mrs. Gray thought it wasn't so ugly after all. She could not believe the attraction that old truck had. It had become synonymous with Gray's Magic Creations. A light bulb came on in her brain! Gray's Magic Creations. GMC! She would talk to her husband, and Silas, when he came home from the big track meet.

Silas didn't do very well in the debate. Maybe he was nervous. No, he told himself he had done this countless times. Maybe his mind kept wandering toward Paula. She, however, excelled, coming in first. Silas was proud of her and found himself wishing he could afford something nicer to take her out in. The GMC ran fine. He only thought something with a bit more creature comforts would be nice. However, he was thankful for the truck, and Paula didn't complain.

A week after the debate, at the next track meet, Silas wasn't nervous at all. He shifted his weight from foot to foot and limbered up. The stands were packed with students from both schools. Silas knew Paula was up there. He really paid no attention to the other runners. This was the last event. Take this and one more trophy for our school. He dropped, foot to the block, awaiting the starter. Concentrate. Stay focused.

The shot rang out and he was off. His feet dug into the cinders as he chased down the boy in the other school's colors. His lungs felt as though they would burst. He didn't know if he could do it, and then the chanting started. Pinky! Pinky! Pinky! Paula would be one of those chanting. His lungs bursting, he pushed harder and pulled ahead. Just barely, but he crossed the line first. The stands erupted in cheers! Well, those from our school.

Silas arrived home with the team and a hero's welcome. There was a write-up about the meet and Silas' come from behind victory.

After a celebratory dinner with their son, the Grays sat down with him to discuss a business proposition. Mrs. Gray, who had said the GMC was so ugly, now wanted it! She and Silas's father found the truck to be a veritable gold mine in advertising. They wanted to put it in the shop and have it professionally painted a jelly bean pink with Gray's Magic Creations lettered in candy cane stripes. They told Silas they would buy him a suitable used car. Silas, of course, accepted.

They took him car shopping the following afternoon, and Silas picked up Paula in a very nice '57 maroon and white Pontiac hardtop. So much for Pinky.

The GMC came out a shiny pink and drew even more attention. How fitting a life of leisure for a jelly bean pink Gray's Magic Creation.

## Doctor, Lawyer, Indian Chief

It was cold that afternoon as I pulled up to the red light. I looked to my left and saw a '69 Pontiac GTO Judge in Carousel Red. I could see its exhaust in the cold air. The driver brought up its revs and took off. You could tell it was a 4-speed; you could hear it catching gears, though you couldn't see it. I turned in the same direction on my way to work after class.

I caught up with the Judge about two blocks from the hospital. Actually, the police had it pulled over and was issuing a ticket to its driver. It wore an out of state tag, and I had never seen it before. Not that I knew every car in town, but a Carousel Red Judge tends to stick out. The driver was new in town, but would become well known after the next few months.

His name was Dr. James Colbert. He was doing a residency in pediatrics. He purchased the car new two years before. The doctor was said to have loved its looks. He also discovered an addiction to the Ram Air III's power. If you are reading this, you know what I mean. By the following spring, Dr. Colbert had gotten two moving violations in his GTO. He had to be careful; he needed his driver's license.

He moved to an apartment on the east side and set about serving his residency. Things were going well. His apartment was on the twelfth floor and had a commanding view of the riverfront. When he was home, that is. The hospital kept him busy; sometimes he would not see his home for days. He didn't have much time to socialize, though he had noticed that a very pretty redhead had recently moved into his building. A few times they had passed in the hallways on coming and going, or at the elevator. The young doctor would have liked to get to know her. He would get his wish.

Dr. Colbert was on his way home one evening after a grueling stint at the hospital. He was almost home. He had caught third and the Judge was doing its thing. Red lights filled his rearview mirror.

For the good doctor, it would prove to be the straw that broke the camel's back. He was arrested and the GTO impounded. The doctor bonded out and was given a date to appear in court. He could not get the Judge back until morning. What a way to start the evening!

He had made an appointment with an attorney and several days later sat in the waiting room. He could not help being nervous. He was facing the revocation of his license.

Finally, the receptionist said he could go in. He entered and was speechless. It was her! The redhead from his apartment complex. Well, at least now he knew her name: Rhonda McMinn.

"Well," he smiled. "I had no idea you were an attorney, nor did I know your name."

She sat down at her desk and smiled in return. "I had a pretty good idea who this was about. This town doesn't have very many doctors terrorizing the streets in orange cars," she said. She went on to say it was going to be a hard fight. He had gotten too many tickets in a short period of time. She promised to do her best and asked if he could try to slow down.

The doctor did some research on the counsel

defending him. She was three years his junior and had only recently joined the law firm. She drove a '70 Grand Prix in a shade of green that reminded him of her eyes.

Once all of this was over, he would see if he could get a date with her...if he still had a license.

Dr. Colbert was extremely busy during the two weeks leading up to his court date. He had looked into his options should his license be suspended. Cars and buses were his only options. Miss McMinn gave him a rough idea of how long it could be suspended. He vowed to take it easy, keep his foot out of it...when all of this was over. Right now, he was needed in ER.

He picked up his messages on the way out the following morning. His court appearance had been postponed. The judge (court, not Pontiac) had some kind of emergency in his family. He started his car and eased onto the street. Oh, well, at least he would have his license a bit longer.

The doctor was called to the hospital at four in the morning. It was 5:30 in the evening by the time he finally arrived home, and pulled the GTO into the underground parking of his complex. The idle of the 400 ricocheted off the walls. It was then his counsel, Miss McMinn, approached him. She had just gotten home herself.

"So, this is the reason you need representation," she said. She also told him why the court date had been delayed. The judge he was to go before had been at the hospital. It seems his granddaughter had been admitted to the hospital a week ago. She had suffered a ruptured appendix and nearly died from infection. She only now was taken off the critical list. She would be okay. The bad news for Dr. Colbert was that his court date was now set for Monday.

His mind raced. Was his granddaughter nine? He

mentioned a name. Was that it? The lead-foot doctor had been her pediatrician. Still was. Yes, he assured her, the girl will be fine and should be able to go home by Saturday.

Miss McMinn and Dr. Colbert stood before the bench that Monday morning. The judge shuffled some papers and removed his glasses. He was aware of the identity of the man before him, the man who had saved the life of his granddaughter. He couldn't just let him off. He had to mete out justice. It was blind after all. Finally, he addressed the doctor.

"Young man, Dr. Colbert. The court finds you guilty of the charges before you. By all rights, your driving privileges should be suspended. However, that would place a burden on the citizens of our community. In light of that, you have a choice to make - that car or your license. To keep your driving privileges, you must not drive that car for a period of one year." And he dropped the gavel.

Dr. Colbert was stunned! He still had his license, but the GTO was doing a year in solitary confinement!

His honor thanked him for what he did for his granddaughter and reminded him that if he were caught behind the wheel of the Judge, his license would be revoked. Dr. Colbert placed his beloved Pontiac in storage for a year. He then purchased a set of inexpensive wheels to get him around. It would be a long year, but he vowed to go easy on it once the time was over. The doctor did ask Rhonda out, and she accepted. A year and a half later, they married and went on to raise two children.

And the Judge (the Pontiac)? It retired to Florida and underwent a frame off restoration. It takes it easy these days, living in a climate-controlled garage - except for those times the doctor and his lovely wife take it out on the street. There it can be seen holding court, dispensing justice. You ought to see it drop the gavel!

## Ian and the Disappearing Morris

Ian MacEwan's family and my family were friends. His father operated a metal fabrication shop in town. Ian and his older brother, Donald, had grown up around the shop, but it was clear that Ian did not want to follow in his father's footsteps. He had always said he wanted to be in the military. After high school, Ian enrolled in college. He had good grades and even made the dean's list. After two years, Ian left college to join the Marines.

One thing I should say about Ian: you probably noticed by his name that he was of Scottish lineage. Ian didn't care for sports, though he was constantly sought by the school teams. Ian did participate in the Highland games, though. He was excellent at tossing the caber, as he was also quite stout. Ian was five feet ten or eleven and weighed two hundred eighty pounds, not an ounce of it fat. His chest and arms were massive. He, like his father and brother, lifted weights. Once, at the Highland games, one of the school kids laughed at his kilt. Ian's father told the kid, "If a man can throw a telephone pole, you might not want to call him a sissy."

So, Ian sold his 1958 Mercury sedan (he did not like small cars due to his size), and left for Parris Island. Gloria, his girlfriend, was not happy about this, however. Those who knew them wondered why they dated. Ian was ultra-conservative while Gloria was a liberal. She was an environmentalist when it wasn't popular to be one and drove an old Volkswagen convertible. I'm not sure about its age. This was the fall of 1969. Imports were making inroads, and the Detroit auto makers would shortly unleash a fleet of subcompacts.

Gloria promised to write, and she did faithfully. Ian appreciated the letters, especially while he was in Viet Nam. He did two tours of duty. While he was away, Gloria graduated and became a high school teacher. She had also become more liberal in her views. She had moved into a new apartment building close to downtown. The building was a modern, twenty-story building with twelve steps to the glass front entrance. This part of the story will be mentioned later, so pay attention.

It was now 1973, and Ian was home. He was a sergeant and was officially discharged, although he had a certain length of time to re-enlist and keep his rank. The first thing he did was buy a car- a new 1973 Pontiac Grand Prix, lovely in triple black. He paid cash for it with his combat pay. His family told him of Gloria, well, that she had been dating a fellow liberal environmentalist. They were into the anti-war movement, and Ian's mom told him to forget about Gloria. She told him there were "lasses" out there to be found.

Since he had come home, he was even stouter and in better physical condition. He had lost ten or fifteen pounds and was tough as nails. He was tanned, and his red hair was cut very short. Ian had been home three days before he actually saw Gloria. They met for lunch one Saturday. Immediately, Ian could see that his parents were right. Gloria did not like the fact that Ian was going to re-enlist. He liked the military, the structure, the feeling he got from being a part of the

Marines. Gloria told him he was part of the "war machine," and then there was the matter of his choice in things automotive. He drove "gas hogs," while she now had a new Volkswagen convertible. So, Ian thanked her for the letters she had sent him, said that they had meant a lot to him, and he bid her good-bye.

The following Monday found Ian at the Marine recruiting office. He would leave the following Saturday, driving the Grand Prix to Parris Island. This time, he would enter training to become a DI (drill instructor). He spent the days with his family and friends. He ran into Gloria a few times and wondered what he had seen in her. True, she was a knockout, but he and she were worlds apart in every way.

Ian and his brother were going to the movies that Wednesday afternoon and ran into Gloria and Drew, the guy Gloria was seeing. Drew was several years older than Gloria and was also a teacher at the high school. Civics was his subject of choice. He was a few inches taller than Ian, but half of his weight.

His hair was long and pulled back in a pony-tail, and he wore a goatee. His attitude was a bit arrogant, Ian thought. He could sense it in the way this guy looked at his uniform. Ian had seen it before from anti-war protesters at airports. It was a feeling he did not like. Ian held disdain for the teacher, but he smiled and went about his way.

After the movie, Ian and Donald went to the Pontiac in the theater parking lot. On the windshield in white shoe polish was written, "Peace Now - No War!"

Ian was furious! They drove to a car wash and cleaned his beloved Grand Prix. Ian and his brother had a good idea who had done this, especially since the attendant at the service station next door had seen

Gloria and the pony-tailed boyfriend loitering near the car.

OK, Ian couldn't beat Drew up, not that he didn't want to. But he was not going to mess up his career by getting in trouble with the law.

Scots are a people not to be messed with. Ian had two days to plot revenge and he would do so. Ian, his brother and their father spent Thursday and most of Friday devising a plan. Donald had found out what kind of car Drew owned- a late-fifties or early-sixties Morris Minor, a British sedan about the size of an overturned bathtub. The clutch and brake pedals were the size of half dollars. As if that was not distinctive enough, the car was painted aqua and was covered with peace symbols and anti-war decals. It was also determined that Drew had been living with Gloria for some time.

The MacEwan clan gathered at their favorite pub shortly after dinner. Ian did not wear his uniform. They all dressed in jeans and dark shirts. One could see Ian as if reflecting on some night mission in Viet Nam. Only this go-around, they did not black out their faces. No, only a few Black Label ales. Mrs. MacEwan was the designated driver. Around nine thirty, they all piled into her Buick Electra and headed for the enemy's camp: Gloria's apartment building.

The parking lot was dimly lit as Mrs. MacEwan parked the Buick. "All right, lads, let's do it then," Mr. MacEwan said in his heavy accent. The three men found the sticker-festooned, dinky British car. Ian got in front of it while his father and brother took the rear. They put on gloves and signaled to each other. Grabbing the bumpers, they physically picked the car up and walked it to the twelve steps. This part would be trickier - getting it up the steps without getting caught. It was dark with only two lights illuminating the way, and the men had Guiness driving them on.

Five minutes later, the Morris Minor, in all its decaled, sloganed wonder, sat on the landing in front of the double glass doors of the apartment complex. "Good job, lads! Good job," Mr. MacEwan said, as they headed toward the Buick.

The next morning, Ian was on his way to Parris Island in his Pontiac. Meanwhile, the apartment dwellers were tripping over the Morris.

The MacEwans were never questioned about this, though it was common knowledge they were the only people around with enough brawn to put the car up there. I am not sure how Drew got it down from its lofty perch. Rumor had it that Gloria prevailed in talking Drew out of pressing charges. He agreed that if they could do what they did, they may he able to hurt him. Drew wisely let it go.

Ian went on to a distinguished career in the Marines, devoting twenty-six years. And, yes, his mother was right. There was a lass out there for him - Cindy, a lady Marine, who bore him a son. When l last heard, he was also a pretty fair weightlifting, caber tossing Marine.

*Past the Hood Ornament*

## G.T....J?

My freshman year of college also brought a new job, working part time at a local department store. The hours fit my schedule and it was easy. All I had to do was make sure the customers in my assigned department were waited on and make sure the merchandise was stocked. It was a lot different from detailing cars, as I had been doing. I missed the cars, but the store had a lot of girls working there. So it had its advantages.

    I had worked there several months when Jeff started working in the department next to mine. He was not a local; he was from Buffalo, I think. He was a sophomore and a year my senior. Jeff was tall and gangly with blond hair, and he was always smiling.

    Jeff was an education major with plans of becoming an auto shop teacher. He would be qualified, as his dad operated a large repair and speed shop. Jeff had grown up around that shop. He had started out sweeping the floor and soon was learning mechanics from his dad.

    He also was a Pontiac aficionado...but he also had a taste for the, shall we say, strange? When he was sixteen, he saw a 1951 Henry J behind a service station.

    Yeah, I know, a lot of you young guys are scratching your head. There really was a Henry J. Ask your grandfather. It was made by Kaiser. Never heard of that either, huh? It was a small, fastback economy car. Anyway, it had not run in ten years. Jeff paid $50 for it and drug it to his Dad's shop. Over the next two years he rebuilt it. Frame off. Okay, I said rebuilt, not restored.

The car that was in the parking lot now had a Ford 9-inch rear, a 4-speed from a GTO, and the engine came from a '63 Catalina, 389, of course. It had been bored, and I don't know what else. I do know it had a very large 4-barrel and lots of grunt!

The American mags set off the deep green paint job. The interior had buckets done in tan leather, and it had a roll bar! His Dad had taught him to paint, but the interior was done at an upholstery shop.

This little car was done right. It looked like Henry J. Kaiser had built it that way. Here's the clincher--from the factory, Henry Js had Henry J on the hood and deck lid. Jeff had taken chrome letters from a GTO. I think he fabricated the "J" and had placed it where Henry J had been...GTJ! I was in awe. I was envious.

One afternoon, Jeff and I went to lunch in the GTJ. For me, it was a two rolls of Charmin ride. He punched it in first and pulled the front wheels off the ground. They touched the ground only to go back up in second and again in third. This thing could run! That's what happens when you stuff truckloads of Pontiac power in a lightweight tinker toy.

The GTJ was one of the quickest cars in the area, so quick in fact that it could beat "The Paddy Wagon," the police department's '64 GTO racecar, at the dragstrip. The Paddy Wagon was built to help deter illegal street racing and encouraged people to go to the track to try to outrun the police in a more lawful way. The GTJ was one of the few cars that could beat the cop-sponsored racecar, even when the GTO was spotted a multi car-length head start. I must be fair, however. The GTJ was a whole lot lighter and was probably putting out a lot more power.

The GTJ was quite popular around town. As the

## Past the Hood Ornament

Beach Boys sang, "The fast guys knew him, and they left him alone." Jeff wasn't into street racing anyway. Sure, he ran it through the gears to show me what it would do, but, if you wanted to race him, he would see you at the strip.

Jeff wanted to teach shop, as I said. His other ambition was to one day own a new Bonneville. He wasn't interested in a Firebird or GTO. He already had a fast car. He thought they were great highway cruisers. Of course, we know he was right.

One afternoon, a man in his forties came into the store looking for Jeff. He told Jeff that his teenage son had seen the GTJ run at the drag strip and had talked about nothing else since. Would Jeff consider selling it? Name your price. Evidently, the man was wealthy and very indulgent.

Jeff pulled what he thought was a ridiculous figure out of the air. He was shocked when the man told him that was no problem. Jeff was stunned! He told this man to give him a couple of days to think it over. The man took Jeff's phone number and assured him he would call him in two days. If Jeff were to sell the GTJ, he would have enough money to buy a Bonneville. A new one if he wanted, or he could get a good used one and bank the difference. He had a big decision to make. Would he miss the little green bomb? Certainly.

We talked about this after work. I told him he had to do what would make him happy. A Bonneville would not pull the front wheels off the ground, but if he liked the comfy cruiser, go for it. Besides, if he built that car, well, he could build another after he graduated. Right?

It was four days later when I saw Jeff. Indeed, he had sold the GTJ. It was replaced with a beautiful '65 Bonneville convertible in red with a black top. It was two years old and like new. He even had ample money left to put away in the bank.

His old hot rod went to a 17-year-old boy twenty-five miles away. His father, the man at the store, was a well-to-do lawyer who indulged his only son.

November was upon us, and the store was keeping us busy with its seasonal shoppers. Not to mention classes. Jeff was very happy with his big Pontiac. Some of us were truly surprised, but I could understand. Jeff was his own person. Not stamped from a cookie cutter, and I liked that. He liked unusual things, hence, the Henry J. Well, I guess it was unusual for a nineteen-year-old to want a full-size Pontiac. There are stranger things, and he told me once that he built the GTJ as a learning experience. I think he learned extremely well. It served its purpose and he moved on.

December was upon us with its snow and cold weather. Jeff and I were wading through the Christmas shoppers one Saturday morning when the store manager approached us with the news. The young man who owned the GTJ had been in a terrible accident. He did not survive. It seems he had been out with friends at a party. On his way home, he passed a car and hit an oncoming car head on. He was speeding. It was snowing. The other driver did not survive either.

Jeff paled. He had to go sit down. He was so distraught. At first he thought it might be his fault if he had not built the hot rod GTJ. Of course, he came to his senses and realized he probably would have been speeding no matter what he was driving. It was still a tragedy, and very sad.

The good news is that after he graduated, Jeff was hired at the high school as a shop teacher, and though it caused some painful memories, the GTJ was very unforgettable. Kids remembered that car. It inspired them to work on cars themselves. Though I have to tell you, I doubt you will ever see anything like that 1951 Henry GTJ.

*Past the Hood Ornament*

## *The Homefront Chief*

He was a fixture in our town. A certainty. As sure as the sunrise, and had been as long as I could remember. Dr. Herron would wheel through the streets of town daily, sometimes accompanied by his wife, in the old Pontiac sedan. It was a six-cylinder 4-door. It had a simple elegant refinement about it. Its attractive blue-gray paint still was shiny in 1973, and never failed to draw admiring looks.

In 1973, Dr. Herron was 82 years old. He and Mrs. Herron were retired from their general practice office. Mrs. Herron had served alongside the doctor as his nurse since the late '20s. The Pontiac joined the practice new in 1937. It served faithfully as the family car, transporting them and their two children. It had also been used to make house calls, and even though the couple had a new Bonneville, they held on to the '37. They loved it! It held so many memories!

When the war broke out in December '41, Dr. Herron was fifty. The draft board told him he was needed on the home front. The war effort and community needed his services. Since he was a doctor, he received a higher allotment of gas rations, and the old Pontiac still wore the sticker in the windshield. The doctor would not remove it.

I remember as a kid in the late '50s being at the city park one afternoon. My friends and I had been playing and sat down under a tree to rest a bit. Behind us was a park bench. We could hear the voices of the two men seated on that bench. One of those men was Dr. Herron. The doctor was tall and thin. His hair and bushy mustache were snow white. He was always jovial and in a good mood.

This day, his voice intoned a note of something he obviously would not view as a pleasant subject. We heard Dr. Herron tell the other man that, of course, the war had been terrible. He told the man it had been hell on the home front, too!

He spoke of the soldiers who returned home badly wounded. He treated some who would recover. He told of the many who did not. He told of the women who suffered, not knowing the fate of husbands, sons, brothers or sweethearts. He told of treating women for depression. Some had attempted suicide. Some had succeeded. Yes, we heard the doctor say it wasn't much fun on the home front either.

I went home that afternoon and poured a glass of milk and munched on an oatmeal raisin cookie, all the while hearing the words of Dr. Herron. My mom was in the kitchen, so I asked her about the home front and what I had heard. She poured a cup of coffee and sat down with me. Mom told me the doctor was right. Dr. Herron had been one of the few medical personnel in our town during the war. The doctor and his wife were kept busy at their office, at the hospital, and making house calls. Mom told me the couple made a house call during the winter of '42 and delivered my brother. Nick. (I told you about him. The one who made my life miserable when he wasn't busy hanging up my grandmother's '52 Pontiac on a stump)!

She told me that night was almost a blizzard, and she was afraid the doctor might not make it in time.

Surprisingly, she went on, the blue-gray Pontiac made it through just fine. My mother was an avid Oldsmobile fan, but she admitted that '37 was one of the most reliable cars she had ever seen. I remembered those words as I watched the old sedan negotiate traffic that morning in 1973.

Mom went on to say that Dr. Herron was right. It wasn't fun on the home front. Gasoline, rubber and ladies' stockings were either rationed or practically non-existent. Lots of foods were in short supply. She remembered depression was common among the ladies who had loved ones overseas. They feared receiving a telegram or a military representative coming to their door. Then, there was the fear of not knowing. Was he okay? Was he injured? At the time I didn't fully understand. Now I can understand how the women, children and men who were on the home front had a bad time of it.

She said she remembered the wounded coming home. So many wounded beyond description. "It was a terrible, terrible thing...seeing so much...just terrible." Mom then told me how Dr. and Mrs. Herron helped our town. The churches were usually full during the war, she said. Even my mom attended, and ordinarily she never went to church. War has a way of bringing people together, and the people would gather for strength from God and one another.

Remember, there was no internet, iPods, or television then. News came from radio and the newspaper. Churches were sort of a community meeting hall. News was exchanged, both good and bad. Joys and sorrows were shared together. Needs were exchanged, as they should be today. Well, the good doctor and his wife somehow, miraculously, would find much needed supplies and drop them at the churches.

Much needed supplies to be distributed to those in need - which meant nearly everyone. These necessities were greatly appreciated, Mom said. How the doctor was able to get them was never known.

Mom told me the Pontiac itself was looked upon as a symbol of hope during this time. It never failed to make its rounds and would show up with the back seat and trunk stuffed with badly needed items. She said some believed it was charmed. I believe it was engineered to be a Pontiac and was driven by a caring couple. True enough, it always got the doctor to his appointed rounds.

So, as I watched that lovely old Pontiac drive through town that hot summer morning with the lovely old couple inside, I thought back to that talk with my mom. As I entered my car and eased into traffic, I could see the doctor up ahead. I began to think on what I heard him say fifteen years earlier in the park.

As great as the Pontiac was, it had nothing to do with the doctor's care and kindness. (Okay, he had good taste). It was the will and determination of a loving couple who wanted to make a difference. That was what caused them to work so tirelessly during that trying time in our history. They cared! Though he was not in the military, he certainly served his country. He and his wife did volunteer work at the veterans' hospital for years after the war. Every 4th of July or Veteran's Day celebration would find the couple in attendance. Both of their children, a son and daughter, went on to become doctors. The son first did a tour in Korea with the Army.

The last time I saw the couple and the Pontiac was 1975. The doctor and his wife passed away within months of each other.

My Dad told me the son took the old Pontiac and

stored it in his garage. Let's hope the proud blue-gray sedan is being driven as it was intended...and in honor of our Armed Forces, thank them for keeping the home front free!

*life through the rearview mirror*

## One Fast Hair Dryer

It was one of those places that seemed to sprout overnight in the seventies. They called them unisex parlors. Barber shops, beauty parlors, whatever you chose to call it, this was a very nice example. The décor was a cool aqua green and lavender with piped in music. Very nice indeed. Far from the old barber shops I had been frequenting.

I had been coming to this shop since arriving in town to start college three years earlier. The person I came to see was a young lady perhaps three or four years my elder, twenty-five at the most. She was a pretty, blue-eyed brunette named Brenda Katz, who was called Kat.

I had an appointment for 2:15 and she was late. The manager said Kat had called a few minutes ago, and she was on her way. She told me to to please have a seat at Kat's station.

Kat had been telling me her car had been using more oil than gas, and she was looking for a replacement. The old '61 Corvair coupe, she feared, was about used up. Fortunately, she had been dating a salesman at the Buick-Pontiac-GMC dealership. She told him she wanted an inexpensive car that she could pay cash for. Oh, yeah. She wanted a GTO. No problem!

Her station was near the back of the building, and suddenly I heard the sound of a very healthy V-8 out back. A few minutes later, Kat walked in from the back and stashed her purse. She was so sorry to keep me waiting. That's okay, I told her and asked what the noise was out back? Her!

No, it wasn't a GTO. It was a Firebird. A '67 Firebird coupe. It was a 400, 4-speed, and was like new inside. It needed a paint job, she told me. Bud, her boyfriend, took it on trade the day before. He thought she might like it even though it wasn't a GTO. He was right. She loved it.

Kat finished my hair and I asked if I could see the car. She glanced at the clock and nodded. I followed her out back. She was right about the paint. It was red with matching interior. It sat on Rally II wheels and redline tires. She said the man who traded it had to park it outside. The top, hood, and deck lid looked like...you know how cars with clear coat look when it starts to peel? Only this car didn't have clear coat. It was a bit dull in other spots. Compound wouldn't help. It needed a paint job.

The interior was perfect, as it was under the hood. It only had 41,000 miles, and this was in March '72. Kat said it made so much noise (it sounded great to me!) because the previous owner had put glass pack mufflers on it.

She was happy with it. I would have been, too. She got it for next to nothing, but Bud promised to paint it for her. A wedding present. They were getting married in June. I drove away wondering what had caused the paint to fade like that, and how lucky Kat was to find the Firebird.

I was working at a department store after class and on Saturdays, and once in a while would see Kat doing some shopping. A few weeks after my last haircut I ran into her at the store. She excitedly told me that Bud was having the Firebird painted at the dealership the following week. Kat also told me a bit of the car's history. The man who ordered it had been in his late 40's and planned to drag race it from time to time. It was ordered with 3.90 Safe-T-Track rear end for maximum acceleration and Bud had a folder of receipts for engine work. It had a competition cam, head work and headers. It had been raced a few times until the owner developed some heart problems. The car had turned 13.51 through the mufflers and on street tires.

Not bad at all, and this was two years ago. Kat was all excited. She had mentioned to Bud that she was interested in taking it to the strip herself!

Sweet! That's the first thing that crossed my mind when I saw the freshly painted Firebird 400. I was actually beginning to enjoy getting haircuts! The glass packs gave it an extra deep rumble, of course, and the idle had a bit of an attitude about it.

Kat said she and Bud were taking it to the strip two weeks from Saturday, on Bud's day off. She invited me to come watch her. She was a bit nervous, having never driven on a strip before, although she was no newcomer to standard shifts. I told her that although I had to work that evening, I wouldn't miss it. This was too cool! My barber (hairdresser?) drag racing a '67 Ram Air 400 Firebird. Yes, indeed, one fast hair dryer!

The weather was beautiful that mid-April Saturday, blue skies and cool temperatures, a great day for racing. I got to meet Bud, a man close to thirty whose personal car was a '65 Bonneville hardtop. He was a Pontiac guy and supported Kat in her desire to race. Today she was seeing what it would do. It was what they called an open track day. Kat was on street tires and through the mufflers.

I do not remember her times, although they were

good for a first time out. There was a lot of tire spin, and she decided after four passes to hang it up before she melted the rear tires. It was very impressive, I thought, and had she more experience, slicks and open headers, who knows? Kat didn't run it on the track after this excursion. She told Bud it had been fun, but no more.

A week later, I was back for a haircut and a chance to find out what Kat thought about drag racing.

She told me she couldn't believe the force with which the car pushed her back during acceleration. She liked it, but not enough to want to do it again, and then she asked how I thought she did. I told her she did well for her first time out, and the problem was it wasn't hooking up.

Yeah, I had to explain that one. Kat was happy with the marriage coming up in three weeks, and again thanked me for coming out to watch her run. I enjoyed it, I told her, and I was going to be busy cramming for finals.

I saw her once more at the store when she came in for some last minute shopping. Kat told me she would see me when she returned from her honeymoon, but that never happened. I graduated and moved on, but every now and then I think back on that '67 Firebird Ram Air 400. This tale was the stuff legends are made of. Car people dream of finding an old classic in a forgotten barn- well, to me this was better. The car was very low mileage, like new interior, spotless under the hood, needed paint- but, so what? It was dirt cheap.

You are right. The only way you would find a car like that today is in some old shed. It's for sure nothing like that will cross your path at a Honda dealership. It did once, back in 1972 at a Pontiac dealer…and, man, could it dry your hair!

## Barney

I admit to being a night person. Years and years of working nights have left their mark, so when I was wide awake a few nights ago, I got up and went to see if any good old movies were on. Flipping the channels, I came across one of the stations that plays old television shows. The familiar strains of the whistling of the theme to "The Andy Griffith Show" stopped me. I was immediately transported back to Barney, the lawyer. No, no, no. To the best of my knowledge Don Knotts never did a routine on the show about a lawyer. Allow me to explain.

His name was James Feldman, III. His grandfather and father had the most prestigious law firm in town. The firm specialized in family law, personal injury and real estate law. James Feldman, III bore an uncanny resemblance to Don Knotts, so, of course, everyone called him Barney.

His parents bought him a new car for a high school graduation present. I will say Barney had good taste. He picked out a 1969 Pontiac Grand Prix SJ. It was a beautiful car, burgundy with a black top and interior. It was a 428 and had a 4-speed.

I saw him in traffic once and had to laugh. I thought of Barney going to pick up Thelma Lou! Of course, had Barney had a SJ Grand Prix, he probably would have had no problem in getting her to ride over to Mt. Pilot.

Barney drove the car that summer and left it in his parent's garage. He was off to one of the big Ivy League universities. He did have the sense to store it properly. The Grand Prix was placed on jack stands with the wheels removed. The battery and fuel were also removed. It was then covered. Keep in mind, it was a new car with only a few thousand miles on it. Well, it remained there through four years of college, then four years of law school.

By the time Barney returned and took his bar exam, the Grand Prix was eight years old, with only 2,600 miles on it. Barney passed the bar and joined the family firm. He then purchased a condo and took the Pontiac out of its hibernation. It was truly a time capsule-literally! I can still remember seeing it back on the streets. Until then, who knew he was back?

The lovely SJ, with Barney at the wheel, could be seen entering the parking lot of the Feldman Law Firm every morning. Secretaries and clients were fortunate enough to hear the 428 announce its arrival.

Young Barney had been practicing for a short time when he met Mrs. Miller. She had made an appointment to seek counsel concerning a divorce. The two senior partners had assigned her to Barney. Mrs. Miller was in one of those May-December marriages. She was maybe 34, while Mr. Miller was 74 or 75. If you are wondering what attracted her to her husband, the answer is, well, money. Mr. Miller had quite a bit of it, and after four years Mrs. Miller wanted her freedom and her share of his very large bank account.

Rumor had it that when Mrs. Miller entered Barney's office, he was speechless, like Barney Fife in the presence of Thelma Lou. You see, Mrs. Miller was stunning! I had seen a picture of her in the paper once.

She looked a lot like Elizabeth Taylor. I'm sure you will agree that Liz Taylor was an all together beautiful woman.

Before long, rumors began to circulate about Barney and Mrs. Miller seeing each other. You are kidding, right? Barney Fife and Liz Taylor? The town laughed at the thought of such an improbability. The rumors and sordid talk did not escape the ears of James Feldman, I and II. They called Barney into the conference room for a serious discussion. Barney was reminded of what scandal, or even the appearance of scandal, could do to their reputation. He was reminded again how old the firm was and its standing in the community. He was also reminded of the code of ethics, which forbade crossing certain boundaries with clients. Barney assured them nothing untoward was going on. They were relieved. I think. Like the rest of the town, they thought...Barney and Liz Taylor?

It has been written throughout the ages that love is blind. She was beautiful. Maybe she had a thing for Don Knotts. Obviously, she saw something in Barney that most didn't. I would like to think he had a kind, gentle nature about him. Having never met him, I can only guess you would like to think the stereotypes are just that. Mrs. Miller did see some quality in him that others didn't, but Barney was teased a lot. Barney was not an imposing figure. He had a good sense of humor, but mostly was quiet and reserved. Did I mention his great taste in cars?

The divorce proceedings, though uncontested by Mr. Miller, lasted almost a year. During this time, Mrs. Miller and Barney would have their clandestine meetings. They would be seen at elegant restaurants one hundred miles away. They would frequent the upscale clubs. Mind you, a couple who look like Elizabeth Taylor and Don Knotts certainly would not be inconspicuous!

Mr. Miller offered no resistance to the divorce. The men of our fair city would say they would fight the devil himself for the stunning Mrs. Miller. Well, okay, maybe, were you not forty years older than she. Maybe if you did not have children who were old enough to be her mother. Maybe if those children were not afraid the lovely woman would leave you penniless.

Back in the day, they would have used a term for all of this...well, maybe two. Shocking! And, scandalous! And, the former Mrs. Miller wound up the wealthiest divorcee around.

The scandal seemed to hit the stately Feldman Law Firm. Barney's father and grandfather were furious at the young lawyer. They, the firm, were the talk of the town. How could James Feldman, III have brought such disgrace to the honored name of Feldman? And with an older gold digger.

Oh, so that's how it was going to be! Well, Barney thought, she was only five years his senior. Gold digger? Had not these two older attorneys built their hallowed reputation by doing just what she had done? What a bunch of hypocrites, he thought. Barney was extremely angry! He turned on his heel and headed for his beloved Pontiac.

He drove around for a while and wound up at his condo. Entering from the garage, his phone was ringing. The former Mrs.Miller! She had called the office and was told he was not in. Yes, of course, she could come over.

I can only speak here from speculation. It was said they spent the afternoon together devising a plan of action. They were in love. Yes, I have touched on that already. Is it for us to question these things? Live, love, and be happy.

Step 1. They drove one hundred miles away and that weekend they married. Yeah, yeah, I know. When word got back to our town, there seemed to be a collective..."Barney?"

The couple spent two weeks in an exclusive hotel. Upon their return, I have heard that Barney did not even say good-bye to his stuffy family. Evidently, he may have looked like Barney Fife, but he was his own man- and he had made up his mind.

Step 2. They disappeared. The Grand Prix and Liz and Barney were gone. This had the town talking! Some said Barney wanted her for the same reason she had wanted old Mr. Miller. Me? I don't think so. I am sad I never met either of them. I think Barney had pride-a fire inside, if you will. He did not like living in the shadow of his family. He wanted to make it on his own. His lovely bride would agree that he was a very good attorney.

No, I don't think Barney married her for money. I think he loved her, and she him. Where did they go? Who knows? Who cares? You see, when "The Andy Griffith Show" comes on, I shut out the whistling and I hear the rumbling of a 428. Squint real hard and you can see a lovely '69 Grand Prix SJ with Barney behind the wheel and Liz Taylor in the passenger seat. It's g-o-o-o-d!

*Past the Hood Ornament*

# THIRD GEAR

*Life through the rearview mirror*

## The Boss's Daughter

I was young and still a newlywed when I entered the hallowed halls of corporate America. The first real job! The job that guys get that finally allows them to venture out on their own and really establish themselves.

It was in those halls that I became aware of Lila. Don't get ahead of me. Lila was the boss's daughter and seventeen. She was used to having her way, a condition brought about by being the only daughter of a wealthy man.

She would from time to time stop by to visit daddy. Yeah, the girl was spoiled. Her outfits probably cost more than what I earned in a week. Her hair and nails always were salon-fresh. You know she could not be seen driving just any car off the economy car lot, could she?

When Lila obtained her license a year earlier, her mother bought a new '74 Grand Prix and gave her daughter her old car. Note, old being subjective here. The old car was a '72 Luxury LeMans. This was a red with white top and interior that was barely broken in.

Now seventeen, she found herself wanting a new car. Her dad argued the LeMans was only two years old. Why did she need a new car? She didn't. She *wanted* a new car. The boss's daughter had grown very fond of mom's Grand Prix and she, Lila, had found a lovely

Grand Prix at the dealership. Please, daddy? Her dad said no. She had a perfectly good car. Case closed!

Not really. Let's look at this objectively. You would think a man old enough to have a seventeen-year-old daughter, plus two sons away at college, a respected businessman, would know better. Lila talked to mom about this.

The boss was a traditionalist. He drove a black Sedan De Ville and wondered why the women in his life were Pontiac fanatics. (Otherwise, he was a good guy to work for!)

The following few weeks were touchy at work. He had a spoiled daughter and wife on his back and he was in a foul mood. Rumor had it that he worked late for at least a week. He probably did not want to go home.

I was leaving the building one Friday afternoon, and as I approached the parking lot, I encountered -- you guessed it--Lila! She was standing beside her father and mother and the black Cadillac. Lila was perfectly dressed and coiffured. The wind carried the scent of her perfume. Beside her was a cherry burgundy Grand Prix. A '75.

The mood around the workplace returned to normal. This was undoubtedly due to the boss's return to domestic tranquility. Lila began to frequent the business again, usually when her purse was low on funds.

On these occasions, I once or twice had a chance to get an up close look at this lovely Grand Prix. I was so taken by the color. It was a unique shade of candy cherry burgundy. I have never seen another and am unsure if it were a special order. I do know it was a great car! It also was equipped with T-tops. A walk around it revealed excessive rear tire wear and paint chips on the lower quarters behind those worn tires.

Could it be that she was flogging the GP?

The Grand Prix had only been with Lila two months when she received her first ticket, for going 50 in a 30 mph zone. The ire of her father got her to take it easy. For a while.

Mid-October marked Lila's sixth month of Grand Prix ownership (well, okay, her father's) and the date of the "incident". Ah, yes, the incident. Lila and her best friend were at one of the burger stands one Friday night celebrating their nearby school's victory in a football game. The spirits of the kids were high. They were proud of their school and were getting a bit boisterous, though the worst indiscretions were the kids leaving the parking lot in plumes of tire smoke.

Which brings us to Lila and her friend. The Grand Prix pulled onto the street with its four barrel wide open and providing bunches of tire smoke! (This explains the paint chips and thinning rear tires)! A city policeman going the opposite direction hit his light and did a U-turn after her.

Lila would later say that she was afraid of what her dad would do...not the police. She sped away and the police followed, for ten miles through city streets. On one stretch, she was clocked at 80 before pulling over, but not before her best friend and passenger decided to remove the T-top panel - in a car that is moving at 80 miles per hour! Valedictorian material, right? A veritable Rhodes scholar!

The wind caught it and, fortunately, the cruiser swerved in time to miss its shattering all over the street. Young "Thelma and Louise" were handcuffed and taken to jail. The Grand Prix, minus one T-top, was impounded.

The boss did not come in on Monday. To say he was furious would be an understatement. I don't know about the girl genius who lost the top panel, but Lila spent the night in juvenile detention. Her dad was so angry that he told his wife that there would be no attempts to free her any sooner. It was time for her to learn a lesson! Lila's mother agreed, though she was understandably upset. She knew her husband was right. Their two sons had never gotten into trouble and it was time to act!

Things were different when Lila returned from her stay at jail. First, she had gotten her license suspended. Her parents were weighing what to do with the Grand Prix, which was still on the impound lot. Second, the boss retrieved the car and replaced the tires, as well as the missing top panel. He had to do it for the sake of his daughter. It wasn't easy to do, but, the Grand Prix was sold!

Lila was not seen much around the workplace after Daddy sold her car. She had been sentenced to community service along with the license suspension. She was doing her service at the children's home, and much to everyone's amazement, loved it! The spoiled rich girl who was always freshly manicured and coiffured, was having the time of her young life, rolling around and getting dirty with a bunch of little kids!

Lila stayed on as a volunteer when her sentence time was served. She had spoken with the administrator and decided she would like to work in this field. She was advised to become a sociology major, which is what she planned to do the following September.

The transformation in Lila was miraculous. Maybe all she needed was a sense of direction, and she found it with the kids.

She left for college that fall with her reinstated license. The car had to wait until her sophomore year. Once she had proven herself, her mom passed on to her the '74 Grand Prix. This car was only two years old. It was silver...and had no T-tops.

They say it served her well through college, and when she returned, it must have. Lila hung onto it, driving it to work at the children's home where she was a social worker. I only hope she tells the kids not to remove top panels from a speeding car!

## The Grand Farewell

This tale was bittersweet to tell. It deals with saying the final farewell to my good friend Billy. If you have been reading my stories thus, then you are familiar with him. Billy of my childhood. Billy who stowed away with me in our teacher's Pontiac convertible. Billy who protected a little girl so vigorously that his family adopted her. That Billy.

After graduating from college, Billy enlisted in the Navy. He had wanted to fly jets, ever since his dad took him to the airport as a kid and he went up in a Piper Cub for a ride over the valley. Billy was hooked on flying after that and went on to earn his wings. He was assigned to a carrier off of Viet Nam in the summer of '74. In March of '75, just weeks before U.S. withdrawal from Viet Nam, his plane exploded. The explanation was vague as to what, and where exactly, it happened. Was it shot down or did some malfunction bring it down? That is unclear.

What is clear is that it was full of jet fuel and armaments, bombs or rockets, or both. It happened in the air and sadly, there was nothing to send home. So, here I was back in my old hometown to say good-bye. A memorial service was being given at his family's church.

I entered the city limits behind the wheel of my '72 Grand Prix and was immediately reminded of him. Everywhere I looked took me back in time. I turned onto the street where we had grown up. Six houses had stood between our homes. Billy was born in May, and I was born in June. I cannot remember not knowing him. He was more like a brother to me than my own brother. Now, he was gone.

I pulled into his parents' driveway and felt so sad. To think of all the times I had spent there with my friend. In the garage was Billy's 1969 LeMans convertible- left there awaiting his return. His parents were lifetime Pontiac people, especially convertibles. Next to his was a '75 Grand Ville convertible. I smiled as I thought back to his mom's '60 Bonneville, a car we adored as kids.

The service would be held late that afternoon, so I took a familiar walk before lunch, one taken countless times with Billy. I retraced the route we took to our neighborhood school. We had a crossing guard at that time, Mrs. Owens, who was a policeman's widow. We loved her and thought she was hilarious.

She used to refer to the kids as "perps!" We didn't know what it meant, but thought it funny. Mrs. Owens would blow her whistle and tell us, "All right, perps! Line up!" or, "Freeze, perps!" if we didn't follow her command. For a long time Billy called everyone perp, and for a while we called him Perp. His mother showed me a picture of him seated in the cockpit of a jet. On his helmet in red letters was PERP. I laughed and wanted to cry when I saw that. He chose that as his handle, or whatever the military term is for a pilot's nickname.

Two blocks from the school was the street which was blocked off every winter. It was impossible for cars to climb in the winter, so it was closed to traffic. Kids used the hill for sledding. We once dared each other to slide down on the seat of our pants. You could build up quite a bit of speed, but your butt would get very, very cold! It was here that we witnessed Mr. Timmons and the runaway hearse.

At the bottom of the hill was the city park where Billy liked to play baseball. The two of us were a lot alike, with one or two exceptions. I never cared for sports, except motor sports. I would go with him to watch and cheer for his team. These games were usually on Saturdays, and Billy and I would go to the library either before or after the game. As you may recall, we performed our best Shakespeare renditions there.

We both loved to read and later on I turned him on to dancing. Yes, I love Fred and Ginger, and as Fred sang to Ginger, "Dancing Cheek to Cheek." (No, I never did that with Billy!)

We had our disagreements from time to time, but it was little stuff. We had each other covered. In fifth grade there was a kid who sat beside Billy who would steal candy from his desk. You older readers remember the desks that had a lid that lifted up, right? Well, Billy liked caramels and would keep a handful stashed in there. He knew this kid was taking his caramels. How could he prove it? We talked it over and devised a plan.

Evidently, the kid would get the candy before class started in the morning, before we got there. Billy knew he was the culprit because he would see him eating caramels only on mornings when Billy had left candy the day before. Now, I don't recall which of us came up with the idea but it sounded like something I would do. We bought a box of chocolate laxatives at the drugstore and wrapped them in the caramel wrappers. Two days later they were left in Billy's desk.

The next day, shortly after lunch, this kid asked to be excused and headed for the door. He was gone for most of science class...and took off again during geography! My accomplice in revenge was having tremendous difficulty keeping a straight face. We never knew if the thief figured out what hit him, but Billy's caramels stopped disappearing!

As I walked back to his parents' house, I remembered talking to my friend about how he and I viewed cars. He liked them, but not like I do. I told him I loved to drive just for the sheer pleasure of it. I know it sounds crazy, but I would try to become one with the car. Sense it. Listen to the engine. Let it talk to you. Feel the suspension as it works under you. The input of the steering. I found this comforting and relaxing. Not to mention fun.

What was so great about Billy was his acceptance. Maybe he didn't understand. So what? He did not condemn or ridicule. Life was too short to worry about the small stuff.

The service was small- family, close friends, and Linda, his fiancée They were to be married in the fall when he returned from Viet Nam. Only, he never returned.

I didn't sleep much that night. After breakfast and tear-laced good-byes, I turned to the Grand Prix. I knew as I headed out of the familiar neighborhood that this would probably be the last I would ever see it. As I drove past the old school I choked back a tear as I whispered 'bye to my old friend. Good-bye, Perp...

As I entered the interstate heading south, there was no need for a stereo. No, the reassuring bass rumble of the 400 was warm that morning and all I needed. I think Perp would understand.

## Field of Dreams

From the first time I saw Mrs. Sloane, she seemed extremely familiar. She was seventy, short and plump, with white hair that she wore up in a bun. Mrs. Sloane and her husband had been attending church where the wife and I were also going. It was when I first actually met her face-to-face that the light came on. She reminded me of Mrs. Merle, the lady who lived next door when I was a boy.

Mrs. Merle had been a sort of grandmother figure to me and had won me over the day she ran interference for me, that day in 1955, when Billy and I had our pocket money stolen by that bully Edwin. Mrs. Merle soothed our tears with milk and warm cinnamon rolls. Yes, Mrs. Sloane reminded me of Mrs. Merle. Why not? They both had the same personality. They were both devout Christians and they both made delicious oatmeal raisin cookies!

So, it was three months after meeting them that we invited the older couple over for dinner. What we knew of them was that they had moved to the city due to Mr. Sloane's health. They had been farmers and still owned the farm. It was 25 miles away and had been a mostly cattle operation. Mr. Sloane had inherited the farm from his father and would still be working it if not for his age, 73, and his heart condition.

We knew that they also drove a 10-year-old 1972

Pontiac Bonneville sedan. This was a very nicely taken care of car, white, with white vinyl top and blue interior. So, they had good taste in cars, at least.

Friday evening arrived and the Sloanes came to dinner. We enjoyed their visit and company. They told us of their children, a daughter who lived in San Francisco and was a school teacher. They told us of their family, of their grandchildren. They were so proud.

Then, they told us of their son. He had joined the Army after high school and had become a sergeant and was stationed at Ft. Hood, Texas. He bought a 1970 Pontiac Grand Prix in the spring of '73 and drove home for a visit that summer. They said he was being shipped to Germany.

Mr. Sloane said the Grand Prix was still out at the farm. I was intrigued. The Grand Prix is a favorite of mine. Mr. Sloane said the water pump quit the day before his son was to leave, so they decided to let it sit on the carport until he returned. It sat there until 1974, when their son died in an accident in Germany. Mr. Sloane then pushed it back of his house, into a pasture, where it had remained for eight years. Now, I'm thinking, it had not been started in nine years. What sort of shape was it in? We knew it needed a water pump. What were their plans for the car?

Mr. and Mrs. Sloane said the farm was to be sold. Reality dictated that they could not return. Mr. Sloane admitted the Grand Prix was in rough shape and I could have it. Wait! Did he say I could have it? A 1970 Grand Prix? The elderly gentleman once more said the car was rough and apologized. He and his wife were upset over the loss of their son. Quite understandable. He gave me directions to find the car and said after I saw the old Grand Prix to call him. As they were leaving, I told him

I would do so.

It took me a few weeks to psyche myself up to go see it. Part of me didn't want to believe it could really be so bad. It was left behind because the water pump failed. Of course, pushing it into a pasture would not have done it any good. Eight years in a pasture in South Louisiana where the rain and heat can be unbearable would have taken its toll. So it was that I climbed into my Trans Am and set out to find the farm and Grand Prix. Twenty-five miles later I pulled into the long driveway leading to the farm. The house was as described, a white, wooden house with a large front porch. It had been empty for close to a year and the weeds and grass reflected that.

The property was a maze of fences. Off to my right was a large, weather-beaten barn. I walked past the house and its attached carport and through the large backyard. Once I made it to the fence, I could see the Pontiac about 100 feet away from the fence. As I crawled through the fence and a massive patch of briars and nettles, I saw what at first appeared to be a horse. It wasn't. It was a mule coming in my direction. I had no clue as to what to do. I never saw a mule in Pittsburgh and did not know what to do with them.

It walked in front of me and stopped. Should I pat it? It didn't seem to be a threat, other than it smelled terribly. So I patted it on its nose the way they did in the cowboy movies. It seemed contented and followed me to the abandoned Grand Prix.

The Pontiac had weeds around it. Lots of them. It was summer and hot, and though the ground was dry, the once shiny blue GP was buried axle-deep in ruts. Over the years, it had sunk in up to its hubs. The rocker panels and lower fenders were on the ground. The dark blue vinyl top was badly peeling. The driver's door was open, not that it would have done much good to close it. The glass was busted out. The passenger side glass was intact but covered in the same green fuzz as the rest of the interior.

What wasn't fuzzy green had been munched on by various rodents. I could only stare in disbelief. This once proud, lovely Grand Prix was being reclaimed by the earth...and mules! I understand parental grief. I can only imagine the pain of losing a child. I stood there wondering why he just pushed it out here? Why not sell it rather than this?

I turned and started back toward the fence. Yeah, the mule followed me. As I neared the fence, I could make out a patch of thick brush the shape of a '56-'57 GMC or Chevy pickup. What metal that was visible was terribly rusty.

It was a long, sad drive home. I never did call the Sloanes. I was sick over the sight of the car. Mr. Sloane suffered a heart attack and passed away within two weeks of my trip to the farm. Upon his death, Mrs. Sloane left for San Francisco. I would imagine the Grand Prix wound up in a crusher.

Mrs. Sloane was a lot like Mrs. Merle. Again, I'm not being unsympathetic to a parent's loss. I cannot emphasize that enough. And yet...

As I stood in that field 31 years ago, I could hear the words of Mrs. Merle. "Waste not, want not, Mike." I wondered if Mrs. Merle would have pushed the car into the pasture. I knew the answer. "Waste not, want not, Mike."

And this is my venture into the field of dreams, or what could have been. As it was, it was a field of nightmares. Uh, except for the mule.

## Here's to You, Mrs. Robinson

I didn't know Mrs. Robinson very well, and then only from church. She was in her forties, maybe 47 or 48, about a dozen years older than my wife and I. Gina Robinson was a bit overweight and wore her salt-and-peppered hair shoulder length.

Mrs. Robinson was separated from her husband, a successful businessman. They had two teenage children. To the best of my knowledge, she had never worked outside the home. She was understandably going through a very difficult, trying time. Her husband had filed for a divorce. I had never met Mr. Robinson and knew nothing of their marriage, yet I was sympathetic toward Mrs. Robinson and the kids.

During this time, Mrs. Robinson would seek friendly shoulders to cry on. My wife was one of them. Carol has a very kind and loving heart and will listen and try to help if she can. You want proof? She married me, didn't she?

Gina Robinson developed a routine of calling Carol when she was upset or needed someone to talk with. No problem, right? Well, yes and no. Sometimes the phone would ring at 3:00 in the morning and it would be her. I couldn't tell if she had been drinking or was just upset, or both. She would talk to Carol. I would fall back asleep as they talked. After a while, I learned to simply answer the phone (actually, pick up the receiver and hand it to the wife) and go back to sleep.

One afternoon, Gina Robinson came over as I was waxing our car. Mrs. Robinson drove one of the biggest cars I had ever seen. I haven't a clue as to the year, but it was only a couple of years old at the time, 1985. It was a Mercury Grand Marquis, a very large car.

She stopped to comment on our car. Really, she didn't even know what our car was. At the time, our family car, our only car, was a 1981 Trans Am. Mrs. Robinson thought it was small, cute but small. Weeks later when her divorce was finalized, she told us that she decided to change her image, lose weight, dye her hair, buy a new wardrobe, and get a new car.

The latter she sought my advice on. What was the name of our cute, little car again? If she had one, would it attract men? Okay, I could tell her what it was, but how would I know if it would attract men? Maybe. Maybe not. Again, how would I know? It probably would catch a car guy's attention. So, what if it did? What are you looking for? Someone to appreciate your Pontiac or you?

Not to be mean, but what you would have is a neurotic, middle-aged woman who drives a Trans Am for the wrong reasons. Obviously, not my problem.

Over the following month, I would hear about her excursions to various car dealers and the various cars she had looked at. Mostly, we heard about the different colors. No, she didn't know what was under the hood.

One afternoon, I answered the phone and it was Mrs. Robinson. She said one of her kids' friends told her that if she were going to buy, as she put it, a "cool" car, it would need to be a four-speed. What did I think? Now, this was a question from left field. In essence, she was asking me if a standard was more "cool" than an automatic. I didn't think so. Our car was an automatic, but I have owned standard shift cars.

I told her that it didn't matter who thought it was cool. What was important was what she thought. What I thought, what your kids' friends thought, is not important. Besides, could she drive a standard? She assured me that she could, though I had a hard time envisioning her going through the gears of a four-speed. She seemed too affluent, too stereotypical middle-aged mother for me to see her in a Trans Am. Forgive me for trying to paint with such a broad brush. But, see, it's like picturing June Cleaver, pearls and all, behind the wheel of a Trans Am or GTO. Possible? Sure. Probable? Not very.

Early in August, Mrs. Robinson did trade the Grand Marquis. Yes, sometime between 2:00 and 3:00 A.M., the phone rang, and I handed it to Carol and went back to sleep. I learned over breakfast that Gina Robinson had bought an '85 Trans Am. Ah hah! I thought as I munched on my Cheerios. I began to laugh to the point of choking. The image of the little old lady from Pasadena came to mind. Wait a minute! She had a Dodge, didn't she?

A week later, the new Pontiac owner came over to show off her new ride. She had gotten a deal as the '86s were on their way, and this unit had been in dealer stock. Of course, it was pretty in black with lower silver accents. The interior was gray cloth, and it did not have T-tops. It did have full power and air. It was powered by the 305 H.O, which was backed by a 5-speed.

I was impressed with the car. It handled well and had good power, a very nice package. Mrs. Robinson praised the Trans Am's power, though not surprisingly, nothing else. She had owned it not quite two weeks and was complaining about two things. She had not liked the ride, and she did not like shifting gears. Hmmm, you mean, it's not a Mercury Grand Marquis? I'm shocked! Shocked, I tell you!

For several weeks, the phone calls at strange hours stopped. We caught up with her at church, and she told us how busy she had been. Gina Robinson did not have a job, as her ex had left her with the house and a steady income. Finally, she confessed to going to a single's group forty miles away.

What Mrs. Robinson referred to as a "single's group" was a watering hole where divorced people, and those on the make, gathered. A night club. No, it wasn't that refined. A bar. Where I was from, they called them gin joints, dives, or saloons. Think of them as chat rooms, only the room is usually dark and reeks of liquor. Well, you get the picture.

She explained that she had been going there three or four times a week. She said she couldn't just sit at home, could she? Me? I only shrugged. I wasn't going to touch that line with a fork!

Fast forward a few weeks. I learned one morning that Gina Robinson's poor Trans Am had been impounded. It seems she was on her way home at 3:00 in the morning (so, that's why the phone calls stopped) and had been pulled over.

Yes, she was driving painlessly! Unfortunately, the Firebird Trans Am was in pain. Mrs. Robinson almost made it home, having covered almost forty miles on the interstate in second gear! Yeah, I said second!

Somehow, she had gotten onto the freeway and forgot to shift. Forty miles with your foot to the floor in second gear is not good for a Pontiac V-8 (or any other make). The 305 had practically melted, and no, this is not covered by the warranty!

The fate of the Trans Am is unknown. After

retrieving it from impound, Mrs. Robinson was upset that Pontiac would not repair her car gratis. I know that she went back to Ford products. She replaced the Firebird with a new Cougar. It just goes to show that not everyone is meant to drive performance cars- or maybe standard shift performance cars. Here's to you, Mrs. Robinson!

*Life through the rearview mirror*

## *Coffee and Doughnuts in the Parking Lot*

It was an early spring day, warm, as I pulled into the employee parking lot. I parked my '81 Trans Am three cars down from the boss's new '84 Trans Am. Nothing unusual, but as I neared the employee entrance, I noticed a strange car. Strange in the sense that I had never seen it before.

The car struck me for its immaculate condition. It was a 1960 Chevrolet Biscayne 2-door sedan in light baby blue. Of course, I checked it out. A glance inside revealed the factory rubber flooring and taxi cab seats. It had a floor shift, something it did not leave the factory with. It had two exhaust tips extending beneath the shiny chrome bumper, the rear tires were wider than the front, and, yes, it wore the Chevy dog dish hubcaps. It was backed into its parking space.

I went into work and thought nothing more about it-until after lunch, when I came back from lunch to find my boss and the maintenance supervisor in the face of a tall, skinny, red head kid of maybe 18 or 19. From what I heard, this was the owner of the '60 Chevy. His name was Mitch Garner. He was 19 and a new hire in the maintenance department as an electrician apprentice. He was being yelled at, but he had a grin on his freckled face.

I found out later that was his personality. He was always smiling.

His infraction was smoking the tires in the parking lot. We did not have a security guard at this time- he was not hired until 1986. But we did have rules and regulations against doing burnouts in the employee parking lot.

Several days later, I was talking with young Mitch. He was a fellow car guy (only he was a Chevy guy). He liked my '81 and my boss's '84 Trans Ams, and he was constantly trying to get one of us to race his Chevy. We had a few fast cars among the employees, a Corvette, a hand full of Trans Ams and Z-28s, and even a 440 powered Dodge Coronet.

Now, I have been known to engage in a street race or two. However, this kid's old Biscayne was now motivated by a built 454 topped by a Holley carburetor the size of a 5-gallon bucket! It didn't take much thinking to leave him alone. What Mitch had was pretty much a street driven gasser. He told me it had been his grandfather's, and upon his passing it had become his. In the year that Mitch owned it, he had changed the 3-speed to a 4-speed, added a 4:11 Positraction, upgraded the brakes, and added the 454. It had originally been a six, a real stripper. It didn't have a radio. It had no power brakes and, pay attention as this will be noted later, no power steering.

So it went. When Mitch wasn't goading someone into a race, he would smoke the tires at lunch. He would always back his hot rod into the parking space. He would get into it, rev up the raucous big block and dump the clutch. He would then return to face a good reprimand.

The saving grace for Mitch was that he was a natural born electrician. If it was electrical, he could fix it. This did not cease to raise the blood pressure of the two previously mentioned supervisors. Mitch was yelled at, threatened, had his pay docked a couple of times- to no avail. He would always walk away with his goofy grin spread across his face.

Mitch was doing great on the job, other than his flagrant disrespect for parking lot protocol. There was no denying he was a quick learner and good at his job. Mitch was called into his boss's office one evening and told that word had reached upper management about his smoky escapades. He was advised to not do it anymore, or he would be let go, no ifs, ands, or buts.

This hit home with Mitch - for a couple of weeks, anyway. One of those weeks was due to a busted engine. Mitch had been at the strip one Saturday and put a hole in one of the pistons. The Chevy was laid up for a week while the engine was rebuilt, but it returned, meaner and healthier than ever.

The Chevy had been repaired and was back at work for a week before temptation started itching its driver's lead foot. One Wednesday evening, Mitch went to lunch as he had so many times before. The light blue Chevy could not be discerned from the tire smoke as it left the employee lot. Upon his return, Mitch backed the car in and entered the building to be met by two irate supervisors. Didn't he understand the severity of his actions? Didn't he appreciate his job, his future?

He, of course, smiled and promised not to do it again. His boss and mine took a coffee break together and conspired to save this talented young man's future. The two men had their heads together for close to an hour before breaking up.

They went about and asked we employees one by one to move our cars to the far end of the parking lot. Ours was not to question why, ours was but to do or die, no matter how curious we were. We had no idea what was afoot. The boss smiled and said we would see come quitting time.

When it was time to go home, we all went to our cars, which were on the other side of the lot. Mitch ambled over to his car and didn't seem to notice it strange that every other car had been moved. We still had no idea what was to come. We stood huddled together as Mitch fired up the 454. True to form, he revved it and came off the clutch! The rear tires lit up, and the car lurched forward...into a lovely pair of smoky doughnuts!

The hot rod did two 360 degrees before coming to a stop, extremely close to a chain link fence. The passenger door opened and the ruddy-faced teen emerged, ashen-faced and knees wobbling! This was all done to the outrageous gales of laughter from his fellow employees!

It seemed that while we were moving our cars, the boss went to Mitch's and since it had no power steering, cranked the wheel to full lock, and the 454 threw it into two beautiful circles!

Mitch was shaken up, but, not mad. His smile returned with his complexion, and he understood what the boss did it for. For him! To save his job!

Several weeks later, Mitch became a Pontiac owner. He liked the looks of my boss's '84 Trans Am - it must have made an impression on Mitch, whatever the reason - and went and bought one of his own. He had a big payment, but, he was still living at home. He didn't do any parking lot burnouts, and if anything, babied the Trans Am.

Mitch thanked my boss on several occasions. The boss said it was no big deal. He only wished he had some coffee to go with the doughnuts!

## Lunch Break Resto

I walked through the employee parking lot that afternoon on my way to the job. Nothing unusual. I had done this more times than I cared to remember. By this time, I had already been living in Louisiana for several years and I had come to appreciate the climate, which was much warmer than Pittsburgh, where I grew up.

The only unusual thing that afternoon was parked close to the entrance - a '69 Pontiac Grand Prix. It caught my attention for two reasons. It was twenty years old, and I used to own one. Mine had been a light gold with no vinyl top. This Grand Prix was white and also had no vinyl top. Of course, I stopped for a close inspection. The black interior was in great shape. It had Pontiac Rally II wheels and whitewall radials. The paint was dull and chalky, as though it hadn't been waxed in a while. It had New York plates on it, so I checked for rust and was surprised to not find any. As I was kneeling down checking the rocker panels and lower fenders, I heard the familiar voice of a Northern person barking at me.

"Hey, kid! Whadda ya doin'? Get away from the car! Yeah, you!"

I was surprised. Kid? I was rapidly closing in on forty. I stood and faced the voice, a medium-built man of early to mid-70s. He had a bushy, white mustache and matching white hair. Wire-framed glasses highlighted his piercing blue eyes. He wore a security guard uniform, and I had never seen him or the Grand Prix before. Again, he asked me what I was doing, only now he wanted my name.

His name was Jim Grimaldi; he was a retired New York City police officer and new to the area. This was his first day, and I guess he thought I was acting a bit strange. I showed him my identification card, assured him I worked for the company, and also told him I love Pontiacs, in particular, Grand Prixs, and that I at one time had had a '69.

Jim decided I was harmless and he actually sort of took to me, maybe because we were both Northern people, maybe because we both liked Pontiacs. He had purchased it new and always kept it in a garage it. It had almost 200,000 miles on it, but before he headed south, the engine was professionally rebuilt. So were the transmission and brakes.

Sometimes, I would go talk with him during my lunch break. I found him to be an interesting old guy. He was divorced and had no children.

When he found out of my reverence for Frank Sinatra, his eyes lit up! He, too, was a fan and had worked a security detail at a concert in New York City once. He had met Sinatra and gotten an autograph. I was envious!

Jim used to tell me about his days as a policeman and the times he would chase street racers. Of course, he was a Pontiac fan, but he said the Pontiacs were hard to catch. He said the GTOs were really tough to keep up with. He told me about a chase of an armed robbery suspect who was driving an early '70s Trans Am. They caught it on the freeway by using roadblocks.

After a couple of months, I had asked him about the car's chalky appearance. The black interior was spotless.

The chrome was bright, and it was clean under the hood. Jim told me that while the engine and transmission were out, it had been detailed under the hood. It was very clean, and the engine had been repainted, too! He told me that at age 71 he had joint pain and couldn't wax it as he had once done.

I told him that I was a pretty good detailer and, if he didn't mind, I would bring some compound and work on it at lunch. Then I could wax it and have it looking like a proper Grand Prix again. I thought he was going to cry!

"You...you would do that?" His voice quavered a bit.

I told him it was no big deal. We Pontiac guys had to stick together. I told him he would have to watch the dead flies around the Trans Am. They would land on it and slide off and break their necks when they hit the ground. He thought that was funny, but knew my car was very shiny.

The next afternoon, I pulled my Firebird in beside his Grand Prix and told him I would be back at lunch. One good thing about working nights is that you are not bothered by much pedestrian traffic coming and going. Even thought it was night, the lights lit up the lot like high noon.

I was back with my sandwich and Coke and quickly finished them. I got my rubbing compound from my trunk and applied a coat to the Grand Prix. It wasn't too bad and only needed a light coat. It looked like a different car. I told him the next evening I would wax it. Again, I thought he was going to cry. I told him I had a good time rubbing down the Grand Prix. I told him he was on his own if it was an import. He spit on the ground and told me not to worry. He asked if he should have it washed before I waxed it, and I told him that would be fine, and he thanked me again. I kept telling him I had a good time. I really do enjoy rubbing down Pontiacs.

The next afternoon was pretty much the same, except I was now applying Mother's Liquid, and if I do say so, the car was gorgeous. I got behind the wheel and closed the door. It closed like a bank vault door. It was so familiar, like my old '69 and the '72.

Of course, Jim kept thanking me. I'm thinking, how do you explain those old warm memories that flood in? The sound of the 400 (yeah, my Trans Am had a 400, too). The layout of the cockpit. I had to get out before I started to cry.

Okay, I'm guilty. I absolutely loved the '69-'72 Grand Prix. I love the style, the comfort and ride. I love the 400. I have said it before and I am again, these cars are GTOs in a tuxedo! Pure class...and, yeah, they run extremely well! Please hold your cards and letters. I've never met a Pontiac I didn't like. I never met a Grand Prix I didn't like. The '69-'72s are my favorites.

Back to Jim. A few months after the waxing, Jim was off and came by to take me to lunch as payment for taking care of his Grand Prix. This was his idea, as he never stopped thanking me for bringing the Grand Prix's paint back to life. At last count, I had waxed it for him four times.

The ex-police officer drove to a small diner not far from work. I knew I would suffer from this ride as I watched him wheel the lovely Grand Prix through traffic. As he parked at the diner, I could feel it under my skin. Regret. Remorse. The longing for my old Grand Prix. I can barely remember the meal. But as we left the diner, Jim asked me if I would like to drive it. Would I like to drive it? Do birds fly? Can Ginger Rogers dance?

It was like an old friend. A dear, long lost friend. It

felt as though there had been no time away. Then I pulled into the parking lot at work and thanked Jim profusely and glanced over my shoulder as I went back to work. I could feel the hair on the back of my neck rise as I heard it tell me good-bye.

It was shortly after this that I moved and lost track of Jim and his fine Grand Prix. After all of these years, I am now firmly entrenched in fogeydom, and should fortune smile, I hope to own another.

I belong to the crowd that believes that there are cars...and then there are Pontiacs. And I believe Grand Prixs hold a special place in the hearts of Pontiac fans. How could they not?

Now, if you will excuse me, I have to search a few parking lots. Maybe I'll find a Grand Prix in need of a good detailing.

*Past the Hood Ornament*

## *Will She Run?*

This tale was born in an extremely trying time. At the time, we were already living in Louisiana and Rose, my wife Carol's mother, was living in Texas.

My mother-in-law, whom I was closer to than my own mother, was dying. She had cancer, and for a while was in remission. And then it came back.

When I tell people that I was closer to her than my mom, I get the same response. How can you say such a thing? Easily. I knew my mom, and if you had, you would understand. Carol's mom? Starting with the obvious, she had a lovely daughter. She was also easy to get along with, unless I did something to upset her lovely daughter.

Rose had a great sense of humor, and I could talk to her endlessly. As an example of her sense of humor, she lived in an older house. It had what was called an attic fan, one of those big fans that drew heat out through attic vents. I was at her house with my future wife one afternoon when the belt came off. It had a habit of doing this frequently. This meant going into the attic, which was nothing more than rafters and insulation, and putting the belt back on the pulley.

I just about made it out of the attic, almost to the stairs, walking on the rafters when my foot slipped! I landed straddling a rafter. The deep breath I took should have sucked the hot air out of the attic until the following summer.

Carol and her mom heard the thump and were both yelling up at me! "Michael? Michael! Are you all right up there?" It took a little time before I could answer without sounding like Tiny Tim tiptoeing through the tulips. Later, the three of us were in her kitchen having some tea. She thanked me again for going into the attic.

"Michael, I want to thank you again. Are you sure you didn't hurt yourself?" And, as if a light bulb came on, it hit her. She put a hand over her mouth and blushed. "You must have..." and she broke out laughing. She regained her composure and tried to speak again, only to laugh some more. I didn't think it very funny at the time, but I had to admire her sense of humor.

She was a widow, and there came a time when she decided to remarry. First, I need to explain that Carol is from Texas, and so was her mother. Of course, my mother-in-law married a Texan. His name was Rich, and I really liked him. I thought he was one of the most hilarious men I have ever met.

He was the stereotypical image of a Texan, tall and thin, and he was the kind of person a kid from north of Pittsburgh had never met before. And let's not forget his speech. I swear, half of the time I had no idea what he was saying. For example, Michael came out "Mack-ul!" I was thankful for Carol's translations. In Pennsylvania, they had cats. Texans have "ca-yuts". Somehow, Toto, I didn't think I was in Pennsylvania any more.

There was the day we were visiting them, and Rich and his cowboy boots and Stetson cowboy hat asked me about my car's casings-"kay-sins". I was the deer caught in the headlights! Speechless! I considered myself up on cars, but, what the...My car had casings? He thankfully explained, sort of. He was talking about tires, uh, "tars." Rich would never have made it in Pittsburgh.

Somewhere along the way, after Rich married her, Rose was diagnosed with cancer. You know what? Say what you will. I speak as one who has been in his share of fights and brawls, but when I heard that, I wanted to cry. The last time I ever saw her, she was not well at all. I was upset and though she could not speak, she squeezed my hand as though she were reassuring me.

Toward the end, Carol and our daughter flew to Texas to be near Rose. I was very fortunate to have a flexible schedule, plus all of the over-time I wanted. We had two cars at that time. Carol drove a new Blazer 4x4. I had a '74 Trans Am. It was immaculate inside and out, and it was in perfect mechanical shape. You could say it was my other baby.

So one Friday after work I showered and headed west for four days. I would see my wife and daughter and mother-in-law and Rich. We were living in Louisiana at the time, and the ride over there was relaxing, like throwing Brer Rabbit in the briar patch. I was in my element again, becoming one with the car and enjoying it. I have said this before, but it is pure magic listening to a 400 loafing along, not even breaking a sweat.

I looked down and there was Mama Bear, my daughter's teddy bear on the console. Heather left her there to keep me company. Heather, Mama Bear and I agreed, this car was built for covering large expanses of ground in a hurry. Next stop - Texas.

The sun was coming up as I pulled into town. Too early to awaken them, so I stopped at a car wash. No, let me explain! After driving through Louisiana all night and into Texas, you need to wash the creatures from the black lagoon from the car. You see, those swamp bugs are huge and splatter and will ruin paint.

I might add that washing your car at 6:00 am is a great way to meet the local constabulary. You will be surprised how many officers will stop to inquire why you are washing your car so early. They will probably want to know if you have anything in the car that they should know about. Understandable. It did look strange, my having a Louisiana driver's license and plates on the car.

I arrived at Carol's mom's house in time for breakfast with my family. I even brought Mama Bear in with me and, of course, Heather was glad to see her. The plan was for Carol, her sister, and Heather to go to the hospital after breakfast. I would get a few hours sleep, shower and meet them there. Rich would wait and go with me.

As I lay on the bed in Carol's old bedroom, I felt so strange. I guess it's true, you can't go home again. This home was once where I felt as though I was home. But one of those reasons was in a hospital. I fell asleep with a vow to tell Rose thank you for being so nice to me and to thank her for Carol.

I sipped coffee with Rich shortly before heading out. The nap and shower refreshed me. Rich lowered his coffee cup to the table and looked at me.

"Mack-ul. I was looking at that puddle jumper of yours. What is it? A Pontiac what?" I explained to him what a Trans Am was as best I could. He said it didn't have much room in it, and then said Heather's bear was in it. That was funny.

Heather insisted that I keep Mama Bear with me so I wouldn't get lonely while she and her mom were away, to which he replied, "Lor', have mercy." I finished the coffee and it was time for us to go.

Rich managed to get in without much of a problem and had plenty of room for his cowboy-booted legs. This was a '74, so the starting procedure was a bit different than today. Depress the clutch, depress the accelerator a little, twist the key and it came to life and settled into a deep bass, lumpy idle.

Pulling away from the house, Rich noticed the hood scoop move, or shake at idle. "Lor', Mack-ul, what in the worl'?" I explained it was attached to the air cleaner and moved when the engine moved.

The traffic was light that morning and it did not take long to cross the city. The hospital was actually about six miles outside the city limits and was part of the university medical school. We were approaching the intersection which would connect us to the hospital road. There was nothing out there except open pastures and a four-lane road with a wide, grassy divider. This road would also lead you to the interstate.

We were almost to the flashing red light when Rich asked, "Mack-ul. This puddle jumper, will she run?"

I thought this was a strange question. Maybe the stress? Who knows? "Pretty fair," I said. There was nothing coming and only one 18-wheeler in sight. I eased into the inboard lane and at 20 miles per hour caught second and floored it! The hood scoop torqued to the right. The nose reached for the sky and the interior filled with a roar between a Banshee's wail and a sound only a Pontiac can make. Rich and his cowboy hat were pinned to the seat. Third, fourth, and we flew by the aforementioned truck. Way over 100.

Rich picked up Mama Bear, turned her over and put her back on the console.

We were rapidly nearing the hospital, and I backed off, the exhaust doing that delicious snap, crackle and pop. Sweet! I turned into the visitor's lot and found a spot. I got out and went around as Rich got out.

"Well, what do you think?" I asked. Rich sniffed, hitched up his pants and said, "I think as long as you got that car, you ain't got no need for Milk of Magnesia." He turned and walked toward the hospital.

I needed the laugh. Not bad for a "puddle jumper." Of course, she'll run!

*Past the Hood Ornament*

# FOURTH GEAR

*life through the rearview mirror*

## *The Partsman's Backyard*

It was a large convenience store and self-service gas station, one that I frequented periodically for coffee and a great cream cheese bagel. I was in line behind a man who looked familiar. He was maybe fifty with red hair and a sprinkling of freckles across his nose. He was barrel-chested, not much taller than myself. And then I remembered.

"Excuse me," I said. "You work at the Pontiac dealership parts department, right?" It must have sounded pretty lame when he turned around and his uniform shirt became visible.

His name was George Hardy, though the name on his shirt read "Andy." He waited for me to pay and we walked out together. This was the early spring of 1990, and my '81 Trans Am was right out front of the door.

"I bought a center cap from you a few months ago," I said, and pointed toward the center cap on the left front wheel. He remembered me. He was a gregarious, likable guy, obviously a car guy. This was a Sunday morning and his gorgeous, black '79 GMC regular cab was at the pumps. Behind it was a trailer with a '64 LeMans convertible on it. The top was tattered and the dark blue paint was dull and primed in numerous spots. The front end was high; it was obvious it was minus its engine.

I walked with him to check out his newfound castaway. Mr. Hardy told me he found this LeMans in a backyard. The owner had intended to restore it, but we know how the best plans have a way of going astray.

He also told me this was his eighth old Pontiac and graciously invited me out to his place to take a look if I wanted. Now, how could I resist?

I followed him six miles out of the city to a large, old country estate that sat back off of the highway. I noticed under the carport of the neat older house a '66 Bonneville wagon. It appeared to be as sharp as the GMC towing the trailer.

Around back was a large, whitewashed barn surrounded by several storage sheds. Mr. Hardy pulled the trailered LeMans in front of the building and got out. I parked a bit away and neared him as the doors rolled up. Wow! It was anything but a barn! It had a concrete garage floor and had steel beams with numerous hoists. There was a large area on the left with workbenches.

It was an old Pontiac lover's "candy shop", filled with six Pontiacs and one Corvette. I was told this large shop was built in 1970. He and his wife had bought this house in 1965, the year he started working in the Pontiac parts department. Over the years, he would come across a deal that was too good to pass up.

For example, he had purchased and restored in this shop, and they were very well done, a '38 tan Pontiac business coupe and a '41 Pontiac black 4-door. There was a stunning '56, red-and-white Star Chief 2-door hardtop, and an equally fine '63 LeMans 2-door hardtop, also in red with red interior. It was a 326 with an automatic.

There was a lovely '68 GTO hardtop in white (no vinyl top), red interior, 400-350 horse, 4-speed, with air conditioning. It was indeed a great one, which wore its hood tachometer proudly!

The non-Pontiac member of his collection, a red, two top '65 Corvette convertible, was fuel injected. It was one of the few 327 fuel injected models produced in 1965. It was a four-speed and had off road exhaust. It was a very rare and very nice unit.

Sitting by itself in front of a workbench was a solid red, '69 Grand Prix. Its 428 was apart in the process of being rebuilt. The transmission was off at a transmission shop. It had no front end. Andy told me, that he had gotten it from the body shop. It had hit something, which is why the front end was off. The new pieces were in one of the part sheds. This place was a car person's dream!

I helped my new friend unload the engineless LeMans and roll it beside the Grand Prix. Again, Mr. Hardy told me he had plans to put a 455 and an automatic (it had been a 326 with an automatic) from a '70 Bonneville, upgrade the suspension, brakes, and probably physically change the rear axle. He planned to return it to its original dark blue-white top and dark blue interior and maybe add air conditioning.

He invited me in to meet his wife and have lunch as thanks for helping him. Thanks? I was having more fun than I could imagine. Mrs. Hardy, a local schoolteacher, was equally nice. Her husband had become the manager of the parts department fifteen years before. The couple had a daughter away at college; she was planning to become a teacher like her mom.

Mrs. Hardy was also a fan of Pontiacs. They had purchased the wagon new. She liked big wagons and would never sell it. Mr. Hardy said the engine and transmission had been rebuilt at 150,000 miles. It now had 200,000. She had great taste.

I thanked Mrs. Hardy and headed for my own Pontiac. Mr. Hardy walked with me and asked me if I would like to see what was in those two parts sheds. Who could refuse?

As he unlocked the first shed, Burt and Sally came trotting up to meet me. They were two Dobermans who had run of the acreage (which was fenced). He said you did not want to set foot on the place after sundown. I could believe that.

This shed was about the size of a one bedroom apartment and very nice, concrete floor and insulated. Shelves held boxes of new original stock (NOS) parts from the' 40's to '80s. A pallet held the 455 and transmission he spoke of for the LeMans. Four or five engine stands held Pontiac engines that looked like new. No, he said, they were rebuilt.

There were stacks of rims. Some were Rally Is, some Rally IIs. There were even a set of eight lugs. There were various seats, both buckets and bench, some old consoles, and even a few sets of T-tops, though I did not ask what they went to.

The smaller shed held mostly body parts, the aforementioned front end for the Grand Prix was there, still in the original boxes. There were bumpers, fender hubcaps. You name it, he had it. He said he began buying up old dealer stock and interesting parts from salvage yards years before. He even had tilt steering columns and numerous steering wheels. It was great!

He took my number and said he would call me when the Grand Prix was finished, as well as the LeMans. I looked forward to it and thanked him profusely for his kindness, and headed back to town.

Four months later, I got a call from Mr. Hardy telling me the Grand Prix was finished. Did I remember where he lived? Of course. Was I free tomorrow afternoon? Yes. You didn't think I would miss the rebirth of a SJ model '69 Grand Prix, did you?

That afternoon, Mrs. Hardy, Burt and Sally, were under the awning in front of the shop. Who could blame them? It was truly as beautiful and correct as it left the factory except for the addition of more modern radial tires. Andy Hardy knows his stuff, Betsy Booth!

Well, three more months passed before I heard from Mr. Hardy again. He had driven the '64 LeMans convertible to work and asked if I could come see it. It didn't take long for me to get there.

As I pulled up to the parts department, I could see a crowd around the LeMans, its shiny dark blue, Rally I wheels shod with radials. The 455 was definitely not stock. Under the '64 GTO hood was a Tri-Power system and a camshaft swap provided a very lumpy idle. Mr. Hardy had done it again!

I saw Andy Hardy a few more times after that, but, as things have a way of working out, his wife retired, he retired and they purchased an auto parts business/salvage yard in Arizona. Yes, Burt, Sally, one '65 Corvette, and seven fine old - wait, eight! - fine old Pontiacs (I almost forgot the '66 wagon), and one GMC moved west.

Man, to have a backyard like Andy Hardy's!

*Past the Hood Ornament*

## *The Cat Wagon*

I used to frequent a quaint little coffee/donut shop from '93-'96. The main draw was Mrs. Jeri Dale, the sweet, older lady who managed the shop. She made great coffee and pastries She also drove a lovely, muscular '83 Grand Prix.

During my visits in the spring of '96, I would sometimes cross paths with a bright red, '91, GMC extended cab pickup. It was driven by a lady in her 40s. She was either coming or going while I was doing the other. The truck was very clean, but, the personalized plate intrigued me. CAT WAGON.

On my next visit to Mrs. Dale's shop, I asked her about the mysterious lady in the GMC, and the license plate, though it was hard to concentrate while savoring one of those delicious pastries! Okay, you know my secret. I love good coffee and pastries. Back to the story.

The lady's name was Pamela Crochet. She was a divorcee of some financial means. She had no children. She operated a cat rescue several miles outside the city limits. Of course, Cat Wagon! At least she was warning you that she had a few hundred cats.

Mrs. Dale said that Mrs. Crochet had been married for almost twenty years to a very successful real estate developer. His affair with a secretary led to a divorce, and his ex's new-found financial freedom.

The GMC was the first thing she purchased as a

single woman. Mrs. Dale said that she was crazy about the truck, probably because her ex-husband thought trucks were for ordinary people.

The cat rescue came about the same way. Mr. Crochet was allergic to cats. So Mrs. Crochet sort of went overboard now that she was single. I was told that Pamela Crochet lived in a condo (and did not have a feline), and the rescue property belonged to a veterinarian, a veterinarian that she had been dating since starting the cat rescue.

From my seat at the counter, I could see Mrs. Dale's gorgeous '83 Grand Prix. It made it difficult to keep my mind on the cat lady. What helped was I was the only patron in the coffee shop. Mrs. Dale liked to talk when it was slow and I was glad for the lull in paying customers. Had there been fellow caffeine addicts present, I would have missed the following tale.

Mrs. Dale began by stating that she did not know where Mrs. Crochet found the cats. I'm thinking, I don't know either, though there doesn't seem to be a shortage. According to Mrs. Dale, Pamela Crochet had no trouble finding them either.

The previous September, she had pulled the GMC into a convenience gas station. After filling the tank, Mrs. Crochet went in to get a cold Coke. It was a humid, hot afternoon, and she was sweaty after wrangling with rescue cats all day. She stepped inside the store to adjust her purse on her shoulder, removed the lid from the cold drink and took a deep swallow. She felt better.

It didn't last long. The cat lady exited the store in time to see the cat wagon leaving the parking lot rapidly! The petite brunette's eyes widened in disbelief. Her truck was being stolen, along with the three cat carriers in its bed. And each cat carrier held one rescue cat that was intended to go to the rescue shelter.

## Past the Hood Ornament

Amid all the confusion, the police showed up and put out what Broderick Crawford used to refer to as an "APB." 10-4? All right, they did search for the truck and its cargo. The highway patrol had reports of the truck weaving in and out of traffic on the interstate. There was no contact made. No high speed pursuit.

The truck was recovered two days later in the parking lot of a Walmart, 100 miles away. Mrs. Crochet had the GMC detailed and serviced; it was fine. Whoever took it used it for a joy ride. When it was found, it was out of fuel.

Oh, yeah, the fuel tank wasn't the only thing empty on the truck. So was the bed! Three rescue cats were gone. Let's remember, they had been in pet carriers. As our favorite news source says, "Inquiring minds want to know!" What happened to them?

I gave some serious thought to this. What would those super sleuth minds think? You know, Sam Spade, Phillip Marlowe, Joe Friday...Barney Fife? I don't know. I went right to the top. Scooby and the gang! But, seriously! If the young guy who drove off with the GMC didn't know the cats were in the bed, what happened to them?

Cat carriers in the truck bed would not readily have been visible. It would seem improbable that the thief would stop to unload cats, assuming he even knew they were back there. Now was the time for sleuthing of my own. It was known that Mrs. Crochet's GMC was on the interstate and exceeding the speed limit. Could the young thief hit the speed necessary for the carriers to be ejected from the bed? Reality check. I don't think the truck, as fine as it is, will go that fast!

I agree with Scooby and Shaggy. The truck was ditched at a Walmart. The catnapper probably was unaware of their presence. So between the time it was abandoned and being found, the three cats obviously drew attention to themselves...and were lifted from the truck, carriers and all! Another mystery solved! Well, it could have happened like that.

If it didn't happen that way, then after an afternoon of high-speed cruising in the bed of a pickup...well, factor in the rumble of the 350 at speed, air turbulence and who knows? The ride probably took three or four years from the cats' nine lives.

Pamela Crochet, as per Mrs. Dale, still had the '91 GMC, although, it is now retired to the country. A new GMC wears the title Cat Wagon. The veterinarian and Mrs. Crochet became man and wife five or six years ago. She still rescues cats.

I would like to add at this point, gentle Pontiac fans, that I am a dog person. Please put down your pitchforks. The reason? Have you ever spent an afternoon washing, waxing and detailing your prized Pontiac, only to go shower and go to get into the love of your life, and there is a cat on the hood? Have you ever found beagle tracks on your windshield, hood or top? Doesn't it raise your blood pressure to do so?

They left the factory with arrows, Indian chiefs, Silver Streaks, and the art deco amber-light Chief. Not cats! My dog's knew when they heard the 400 rumble- he's home!

*Past the Hood Ornament*

## *Saturday in the Park*

It was a hot, sticky, late June Saturday. The kind of heat that made your shirt stick to your ribcage. The kind of heat that would make non-car people wonder why we would be out walking in a park, admiring old cars.

Yet, here we were. Strolling, sweating through the park, amid a sea of old cars. Every now and then, a breeze would blow through the branches of the numerous trees, providing much welcomed relief. Of course, there were countless numbers of snack stands dispensing cold drinks, but it would take more than summer's heat and dehydration to stop old car fanatics! Right?

I was having a great time. Sweating, but having a great time. Every time I would gripe about the heat, I would remind myself that people paid big bucks to go to a gym and sweat. Hey, I was sweating for free! Oh, well, what a day to get pumped up and buffed.

The car show drew a good crowd, both of cars on display and spectators. As I made my way down the section of full-size cars, the appeal of these old road warriors was captivating. Parked between a '66 Oldsmobile 98 convertible and a '60 Ford Starliner was a '65 Pontiac Grand Prix. It was white with black interior, a very fine example of Pontiac excitement.

Seated to the rear of the Grand Prix, beneath the shady canopy of tree boughs, were the owners. They were a couple in their late '60s or early '70s. They watched as I circled the car and admired its pristine engine compartment. The 389 looked to be showroom fresh.

"Great restoration," I said approvingly. The gentleman removed his cap and mopped the beads of sweat from his forehead with his handkerchief.

"It's not restored. It's all original," he said. He reached into an ice chest and handed a Diet Coke to his wife and got one for himself. "Want a Diet Coke?" he asked and motioned to an empty lawn chair.

They introduced themselves as Thomas and Patty O'Connor. I was thankful for the cold Coke, and as Mr. O'Connor began to unwind his story, I quickly became enthralled in its content. He liked to talk, and I was eager to listen.

He said they bought the Grand Prix new from dealership stock in January '65. It was June of 2000 when Mr. O'Connor graciously took the time to tell me his story. The Grand Prix was 35 years old and had about 42,000 miles. He was 70 and his wife was 69. He was average height, but muscular and fit. He was tanned-even his bald head-because he liked to work in his garden.

He joined the Army in 1948 at age 18, right after high school. Mr. O'Connor spent three years in the motor pool, where he learned to drive trucks. It was also where he became a Pontiac man. He said that he bought a '35 coupe for $15, adding, "You couldn't beat it to death." The old Jeeps and trucks in the motor pool were flatheads, too, and he became a fan of the old straight eights. Mr. O'Connor spoke as one remembering an old sweetheart, and his wife would join in in the same animated manner. They were like two adolescent kids in the midst of a first love.

## Past the Hood Ornament

I could relate to this. Truth be told, maybe you can, too. We older guys tend to get misty eyed over the good old days-those thrilling days of yesteryear! Excuse me, I'm getting off track... Mrs. O'Connor fondly remembered Thomas's old '35 coupe. After being discharged in 1951, he drove it home from California. He laughed as he told of his trip home. "It ran great," he said. "No problems crossing the mountains." The worst part, according to the older gentleman, was crossing the desert. He had to drive at night. What he would have given for an air conditioner like the one in his Grand Prix!

Once home again, Mr. O'Connor moved back in with his parents and began to search for a job. The GI bill was not for him, though he had given it some thought. He had a trade, he said. Uncle Sam trusted him with their trucks and he was good at it.

Within a week, he had a job at a dairy-not as an over-the-road truck driver. No, he was a milkman. Yeah, yeah, yeah. I know. A lot of you young people do not know what I'm talking about. (You wouldn't know what a phone booth is either). There was a time when dairy companies made home deliveries. The drivers wore white uniforms and maybe a bow tie and worked the same hours as the tooth fairy. Magically, milk bottles would be on your doorstep come morning. If you got up for a drink or to make a pit stop, you could hear the rattle of milk bottles, or hear the Divco van with the cow painted on the side, coming up the street.

Thomas O'Connor met Patty at the dairy. She was a new hire in dispatch and worked the same shift. It didn't take long, the spring of '52, before the '35 Pontiac was taking them on their honeymoon, and it was not long after their return that they moved into their own home. The '35 coupe and Patty's '34 Desoto Airflow were traded for a '50 Pontiac hardtop.

Eventually, they had three children and moved to a bigger house. Patty O'Connor left the dairy to be a stay at home mom. With three small kids, the couple bought their first new car, a 1958 Pontiac wagon. I was beginning to think this sounded a bit like a script from "Leave It to Beaver". However, having been there, I know this was mainstream suburban America in the '50's. "Gee, Mrs. Cleaver. That's a lovely frock you're wearing today."

Mr. O'Connor was promoted in 1964 to a managerial position. This meant he was now behind a desk. He was pleased with the new responsibilities and more pay. This is where the Grand Prix comes in. The family wagon, a '61, had just been paid off. Life was good. So in January '65, the couple took possession of the Grand Prix that was within three feet of me.

Mrs. O'Connor said it was always garaged and used sparingly. The family wagon was traded and replaced every 36 months. Not the Grand Prix. It was still with them 35 years later. The kids grew and now had children of their own. Mr. O'Connor retired in 1991 after forty years. Now, the couple spent their time gardening, golfing and taking weekend trips to visit the grandkids. I imagine the Grand Prix would make quite an impression at the country club, and the 389 is a long-legged freeway flyer.

A check of the time revealed that I had been sitting there two hours, and I had a wonderful time surrounded by acres of great old cars, and hearing stories of how it used to be. How it was when these cars were cars. Not appliances!

So I thanked the couple for the cold Coke and for sharing the shade. I had a wonderful afternoon in the park. As I started to walk away, I turned and asked Mr. O'Connor a question. "Do you still have your milkman uniform? Do you ever have the urge to put it on and load the trunk with milk bottles?" I asked, pointing to the white Grand Prix.

A big smile spread across his face. "Well, if I did, it would make it to the doorstep a lot faster than the old Divco!"

*life through the rearveiw mirror*

## Scooby and the Mystery Machine

Old car people fantasize about the elusive barn find, the thrill of finding a "fill in the blank" in an old barn or shed-'57 Bonneville, '69 Trans Am, or your choice of dream car. We picture ourselves as Indiana Jones off on a quest to raid the Temple of the Lost Classic, stumbling upon a rare find under dusty cover, hidden away and forgotten. Along the way, reality hits home. We never will find the mother lode of untouched collector mobiles.

But have you ever thought about those barn finds? At one time, someone parked that restorable beauty in the shed, barn, or garage. At one time, it wasn't lost. How did it become lost?

Through many different ways, actually. The original owner passed away and relatives didn't know the car still existed. Kids grew up and moved away. Who knew about the old whatever? Did they ever care? Maybe. Maybe not. Odds are it was merely unwanted and forgotten. Simply abandoned. Who loses a car?

Maybe some of those were lost purposely. I thought back twelve years ago to an afternoon spent running errands. I pulled into a convenience store and gas station for a Coke. I noticed there were no other customers as I entered the store. A young lady who was no more than twenty greeted me as I entered.

She was obviously bored and stood watching the

passing traffic as I headed for the drink cooler. I grabbed a can and was on my way to the counter when she became excited about something outside.

"Wow! Do you see that? What is it? What is it?"

She was very animated which, of course, caused me to look at what had caused her excitement. In a line of traffic awaiting the green light was a pickup towing a trailer. On the trailer was a beautiful, burgundy '67 GTO hardtop. I could get excited about it myself. I did find the young cashier's enthusiasm baffling though. All right, she has good taste, but, she wasn't a gleam in her parent's eyes when the GTO was ruling the streets. "Do you know what it is?" she asked again.

"A '67 GTO," I told her as the traffic began moving again. "A Pontiac GTO." She watched intently until it was out of sight. A couple of customers came in. I was not going to leave until I asked her about the GTO. Her infatuation, that is.

The customers left and I asked her. For the next 45 minutes or so, between customers, she told me of her grandfather. As a young girl, she would visit her grandparents, and her grandfather would always be under the hood of his car. It was bright red, very shiny. She would stand by him and trace the letters in the grille...GTO.

Her grandmother filed for divorce in 1985, and her grandfather didn't contest it. Her grandmother got the house, most of the savings, and her car. Then, my young clerk said her grandmother's attorney wanted the GTO sold and the proceeds divided. This, she said, was in 1986. Well, her grandfather would have none of this. He and "The Great One" have not been seen since. The girl was almost six at the time. She barely remembered the car, though her dad told her it was a '64.

It got me thinking. Could some of the barn finds,

cars stored away under cover or freshly found cars, be nothing more than fed up divorcees hiding away their stash? While I can't imagine walking away from my children or grandchildren, the way the cashier's grandfather did, blood sucking attorneys and ex-spouses can make you think about it.

Once more, I do not advocate anyone's familial abandonment. Twelve years ago, I went home and thought about what the young lady told me. I think about it to this day. I'm going by the word of the granddaughter. Her grandmother had won everything willingly...up to the GTO. Her mate gave her what she wanted until the attorney wanted his car. It wasn't enough that she had a car. No, her attorney couldn't let him have his prized possession. It was, after all, valuable. Her attorney probably ran one of those ads on television that tell you how you deserve a big cash settlement. Translation- how he can get 40-50% of what you get. What's your ex-husband's '64 GTO worth?

Lest you think this is an anti-lawyer tirade, it isn't meant to be. It is an anti-greed tirade. Think back to the time when the blush of love was on the bloom. Somewhere, someone, for some reason, mortally wounded that love. Part in peace with dignity as much as possible. Call off the attack dog.

The only dog I would call would be Scooby and the gang. For example, a few questions come to mind. The cashier's grandfather disappeared in a red, '64 GTO. How do you hide it? If your ex and attorney are after you, how do you register it? It could easily be tracked. It is illegal to change the VIN numbers, so what would become of the car?

These questions have plagued me for a dozen years. I can't imagine a car guy would strip and sell it for parts. Help me out here, Scooby Doo. Talk about the mystery machine. How would you hide a car like that? Well, any car for that matter. Is it possible that some of these barn finds were placed in those locations due to such situations?

Stranger things have happened. It is not an option I would consider, though. Why park a perfectly good car only to let it sink into the ground? As Shaggy would say, "Zoinks!"

Would it not be better to sell the car, American Bar Association, or not? At least it would not be deteriorating.

I personally would have sold the car, and, I am sure you would have done the same. I know from experience that you can get another. Children and grandchildren are harder to come by. Besides, you can get them to help you restore a likely project. Yes, giving up a prized car is painful. We all know that. Right? Yeah, but I remember that girl from 12 years ago. I don't remember her name, only the excitement in her eyes at the sight of that GTO. She was looking for her grandfather.

Point? I hope there are not cars hidden away for such reasons. What a waste in relationships and of some great cars. That granddaughter should have been enjoying that red GTO with her grandfather.

I need to knock off the editorializing- before I start sounding like Andy Rooney. Now, about those questions I raised earlier. I am going to need some help solving this mystery. I'll bring the Scooby snacks. Scooby and Shaggy, you bring the mystery machine.

## Your Money, or I'll Shut It Off

The idea was simple and began with a chance encounter. I was having lunch at a fast food restaurant, and from the booth behind me heard familiar voices, not familiar as in I knew them, but familiar in style and what it lacked. As a Pennsylvanian transplanted in Baton Rouge, I quickly picked up on the sounds of fellow Northerners.

I turned around and made the observation that they were either from the North, or the only two people in town who did not pepper their speech with "y'all." They were from the Keystone state. They were on a business trip, buying pickups. These guys would buy older trucks and take them to auctions in the north, where they seemed to be in demand. Rust tends to get them in the colder climates and reduces them to rubble. Down south, rust-free examples are all over the place here.

We talked for close to forty-five minutes and they gave me their card. The concept sounded good. Buy a pickup in good mechanical condition, detail it, and take it to auction. Easy, right? "Try it," they said. "Drive it up, sell it, fly home." I would think about it, but it did sound like a great way to make some extra money on the side, and you could work at your leisure.

Yeah, it sounded great, and I would start looking for a truck. This was the spring of '93, and, to be perfectly honest, I was wanting to make a trip home. This would give me a profitable way to do it. I was looking forward to it.

After two weeks of checking auto traders classifieds and scouring car lots, I found one - a 1977 GMC regular cab, short wheel base. Mechanically, it was great. The truck came with paperwork as proof that the 350 4 barrel had been rebuilt. It had been steam cleaned under the hood and looked good. It drove great. The automatic shifted as it should. The brakes and tires were good; even the A/C worked as it should.

Cosmetically, it needed a thorough detailing. It was cranberry red, but very dull. It would take some compounding to bring it back, which I was good at. The interior was also cranberry and could use a good shampooing, and I thought a slide-in bed liner would complement the factory styled wheels.

It was coming along slowly, but I knew it would. The interior was shampooed and detailed and was looking pretty good. It's amazing what some Rit dye can do to freshen faded carpet. Armor All and elbow grease work wonders on dash pads, door panels and pedals. They came out quite nicely.

Polishing the wheels was a little time consuming. I had to use a fine grit sand paper and buffing paste, and finally, apply generous amounts of wheel polish. This was so time consuming because I was doing it by hand and making sure to get the polish into all of the crevices. But the end results spoke for themselves!

Next, a slide-in bed liner was installed, leaving only the compounding and waxing. I thought I would die from the heat! Part of that was my own doing, as I prefer hand buffing. I like to get right down next to the paint and eyeball it as I go. The heat and humidity? I had nothing to do with that.

I called the number on the card to find out when the next auction would be, and Mr. Graham, one of the gentlemen I had met at the restaurant, asked if I had a license. License? What a dummy! I had forgotten that. These were dealer auctions! Before I hung up, Mr. Graham had expressed an interest in the GMC. He knew it would sell at his lot. He mentioned a figure and said if it was as nice as I said, he could go higher. He named a date and asked if I could be there by then. He said he had to be out of town until the auction, but I should call him if I was interested.

I hung up and beat myself up over being so stupid. I'm not a dealer. On the other hand, I don't have to be to find trucks for Mr. Graham. But don't get ahead of yourself. There were two weeks before I had to leave, and I just wanted to make a trip home. If I could find him a truck now and then, fine. If not, that was fine too.

The truck looked pretty nice. Sure, it had some scratches, but it was sixteen years old and someone's daily driver. It spoke to your senses. It was now shiny, as was the chrome. It even sounded tough. The 350 had dual exhaust and sounded pretty healthy. And, it did drive well, although I am not a truck person, so it felt huge to me. I wouldn't want to push it on a road course. To be fair, you can't move a house full of furniture in a Trans Am.

I was counting the days and looking forward to going home again. Actually, I would be within thirty miles of my old stomping grounds and had not been there since I said good-bye to my best friend.

The drive was 1,300 miles, give or take a few, and it would be good to just drive again, just to be driving (though I had never done a trip like this in a truck).

It had rained the night before I left, and it was already dry by 7:00 A.M. Summer heat does that down here. I had an overnight bag on the seat, a full tank of gas, and the Sinatra station on the stereo. Set the A/C, and I was ready. As the GMC left Baton Rouge, I glanced in the rearview mirror. The skyline here was a lot different than Pittsburgh. Would I recognize my hometown now? Are the steel mills and foundries still there? If they were, would they be United States Steel Corporation, or a foreign-owned concern? We are almost out of the manufacturing industry. What's next?

As the GMC rolled through Mississippi, I thought back to some memories of snow, the way it would turn colors in different settings. When first fallen, of course, it's snow white. Walk the streets of a mill town, and it seems gray from the ash and coal dust. On a bright, sunny morning with the sun's reflection, it would appear to glisten so that it would give you snow blindness. The snow would sparkle like diamonds. Under the moonlight, it would have a pale blue iridescence. Lovely!

Entering Alabama, I was looking for a stop. I put the thought of snow aside and began looking for a gas station. The GMC didn't need to stop. It had plenty of fuel, but I needed some. A Coke would hit the spot. I kept going, finally stopping at a convenience store and gas station on the Tennessee border. I pulled up to the pump. When I turned the truck off, the engine backfired. Loudly. It sounded like an explosion. Fortunately, there were no other people filling up at the pump to be startled.

Why had it backfired? It fired right up and seemed to idle all right. Timing must be off a little. It was running strong, had fresh oil and coolant. I would go on.

The GMC liked to cruise at 70 mph, and I think I was adjusting to sitting up so high. This was an easy vehicle to drive, not demanding, but I decided to stop for the night just on the edge of Nashville. How to shut it down without waking the neighborhood? Parking at the far end of the lot helped.

I was up early and, after a shower and breakfast, was on my way again. Might as well fill it up before leaving town, so I started looking for a station. On my right just ahead was an Exxon station.

The station had four pump isles and a canopy covered the area. The morning traffic was still fairly heavy, but there were only two cars at the pumps, a Honda and a 15-passenger Dodge van. The van belonged to a church, according to its lettering on the side. It was on the far outside isle. A tall man in a suit and a tie stood filling its tank.

The young lady in the Honda pulled onto the streets as I pulled the GMC up to the isle one over from the church van. Maybe the preacher, or whoever, wouldn't notice the truck's backfire. One can hope! Of course, it backfired! The canopy only magnified the resonance of what could have been mistaken for a .45 round going off. The guy with the van dropped the hose. Thankfully, it automatically shut off. The van attendant did a bit the Keystone Cops would be envious of! I had no idea a man could run that fast while wearing a suit!

While filling the GMC, I saw him looking from around the station.

"It just backfired!" I yelled.

It must be hard to regain your dignity after such an incident. He straightened his tie and resumed pumping his gas.

Me? I figured I should get the pickup to Pennsylvania as fast as possible. Next fill up, they may fire back.

*Past the Hood Ornament*

## *In Good Hands*

I think it was Yogi Berra who said that you could see a lot simply by looking. I may be wrong. It may have been Boo Boo. I do know that when l was a kid, my dad used to say something similar. Pay attention to those around you and you will learn from them. Listen to what they say and watch what they do. Fascinating advice, and I have been following it since I was but a child.

l was reading an old car magazine the other day which brought this to mind. Of course, you know this was connected. Right? I read about a car that reminded me of one that I had seen 20 some odd years ago, and with your permission...

It was early April 1991 and I was on my way home from a trip to Texas. It was roughly 7:00 in the morning. I was close to the Louisiana border and hungry, so at the next Golden Arches sign I made a pit stop.

The McDonald's was just off the interstate and not very busy, and I noticed the car right away. It was lovely! A 1967 Firebird 400 convertible! It sat in front, where it could be seen from the dining room. The medium blue paint gleamed in the morning sunlight. The top was down, revealing a perfect matching-shade interior. The console indicated it was an automatic. This Firebird looked as though it rolled off the showroom floor that morning! The only indication to the contrary? The Rally IIs had redline radial tires.

I pulled in beside it, and as I walked into the restaurant, I became aware of an older gentleman watching me. He was in his mid-sixties; his still dark hair was close cut and thin on top. He carried himself in the way of a businessman, especially when he peered at you over the top of his glasses. I stopped at his booth.

"Is it yours?" He nodded and we spoke for a few minutes. When he found out that I was passing through and harmless (relatively so, at least), he invited me to sit with him while I ate my Egg McMuffin. His name was Cameron Snyder, and I learned he was 67 and had a story to tell. He was glad to talk to someone who appreciated his Firebird. He had time and I could spare some of mine, and he told his story.

Mr. Snyder began by telling me that he bought the Firebird in 1971. It was bought when his divorce had been finalized. As he spoke, you could sense bitterness and pain in his voice. He said they had been married 20 years and had no children. Mr. Snyder had been an insurance agent, and a very successful agent at that.

Maybe that was why she left, he mused. He said he put in long hours at the office. They had a big house and the trappings that go with monetary rewards, and yet one day he came home to find her asking for an end to the marriage. His wife had someone else in her life. The court gave her the house, car, and half of their savings.

Mr. Snyder had been living in an apartment, and now he found himself in need of a car. The former man and wife had been Oldsmobile drivers, though Mr. Snyder had been a secret Pontiac admirer. He found the '67 on the Pontiac dealer's used car lot, and it was love at first sight. It served as his daily driver for sixteen years. It then underwent a full restoration.

Immediately after the divorce, Mr. Snyder threw himself into his work and eventually opened a second office in a neighboring town. He said that he never trusted a woman with his heart again. There had been a few girlfriends in the last 20 years, but he couldn't get past the memories.

Mr. Snyder bought a small place in the country five years after the couple split. By then, he was financially set and his fondness for first-generation Firebirds also was set. He purchased a '69 400 convertible shortly after moving to his home in the country. The mention of the '69 convertible spread a smile across his face. The car was in excellent mechanical condition, having been recently gone through. It needed paint and a bit of body work.

I was enjoying listening to Mr. Snyder's story. I find tales from older car aficionados extremely interesting. Yet I was getting mixed signals from him. Maybe that's the wrong term. Simply put, talking to him was like talking to two different people. I do not mean he was mentally ill. No, that wasn't it. When he spoke of his old Firebirds, he was like the proverbial kid in the candy store. We know how that is, don't we? Any reference to his ex-wife brought dark shadows to his eyes. He was still in love with her. I am no Dr. Laura or Dr. Phil, but it dawned on me while he described the '69. It gave him something to do to occupy his time.

Mr. Snyder told me he worked on the '69 over two years. He learned to do the necessary body work and even painted it in his workshop. By the way, it was finished in burgundy with white top and interior. I thought if it were as nice as the '67, it would be a fine example of a GM F-body. Mr. Snyder had said it was authentic, plus it was Ram Air equipped.

Sigmund Freud would have been proud of my diagnosis of Cameron Snyder. See, Mr. Snyder told me as much. He admitted that after the '69 was completed, that he needed another challenge. If you guessed that he found another car, well, you are right. This time, he found a '68 400 convertible and had it shipped in from the northwest.

He told me that it had been wrecked and had sat for six years. He knew it need a lot of work, but he didn't care. This was his therapy. It took a bit over five years of working in his spare time. The result of his five years was a Verdoro Green convertible with a tan top and interior. Don't forget, he now had one of each year Firebird 400 convertibles. I was envious!

When I met him, he was 67 and had retired two years earlier. So how did he plan to spend his retirement? Driving his Firebirds, of course. If that wouldn't keep him busy (it would me), he had recently bought a '67 OHC-6 Firebird convertible in need of restoration.

We walked out together and I thanked him for his time. It would have been worth it just to hear the 400 idle. He waved and left. I headed east on the interstate.

I kept thinking of Mr. Snyder. After 20 years, he still loved his ex-wife. His eyes said as much. Sad, really sad. I do know that the insurance agent's divorce was a boon to first-generation Firebirds. They are in good hands!

# About the Author

Mike Carmichael writes a regular car column, *A Glance Back*, which appears monthly in *Smoke Signals Magazine*. He lives in Baton Rouge, Louisiana where, he says, he's "living the dream."

*life through the rearview mirror*

You might also enjoy these fine books from:

## WordCrafts Press

Never Run a Dead Kata
*Lessons I Learned in the Dojo*
by Rodney Boyd

Morning Mist
*Stories from the Water's Edge*
by Barbie Loflin

What the Dog Said
by Joanne Brokaw

End of Summer
by Michael Potts

Illuminations
by Paula K. Parker & Tracy Sugg

www.wordcrafts.net

www.ingramcontent.com/pod-product-compliance
Lightning Source LLC
Chambersburg PA
CBHW071930290426
44110CB00013B/1547